CLINICALLY DEAD IN NEW YORK

CLINICALLY DEAD IN NEW YORK

MIRACLE OF SURVIVING A HEART ATTACK AND OTHER NEAR MISSES

G. OFORI ANOR

ISBN: 978-1-63821-044-3 (Paperback Edition)
ISBN: 978-1-63821-045-0 (Hardcover Edition)
ISBN: 978-1-63821-043-6 (E-book Edition)

Book Ordering Information

Phone Number: 315 288-7939 ext. 1000 or 347-901-4920
Email: info@globalsummithouse.com
Global Summit House
www.globalsummithouse.com

Printed in the United States of America

To Papa Anor and Mena Yaa Asabea
through whom I came, from God.

CONTENTS

FOREWORD

By Rev Dr Moses Biney

"Miracles are a retelling in small letters of the very same story which is written across the whole world in letters too large for some of us to see." - C.S Lewis

In this book, *Clinically Dead In New York: My Encounters with Death, Survival Miracles and Second Chances,* the author, G. Ofori Anor tells the story of the "unseen hand of God" which has many times and in different ways delivered him from death and destruction. These are his "miracle stories". Miracles, as the late British academic, novelist and theologian, C. S. Lewis points out, are very much around us. However, not everybody recognizes them, because one needs more than mere experience to see them. It requires the revelation of God! Those who see the mighty work of God must tell it. This is what the author does here. This memoir captures for us recollections of and reflections on events in the author's life he considers miraculous. Indeed, the occurrences narrated, especially his recent near-death experience, is nothing less than miraculous.

G. Ofori Anor is well known within many circles in the United States and Ghana -- as an exceptional teacher, an orator, a journalist and a go-to person for matters on Akan culture and poetry. His involvement and leadership in the African and especially Ghanaian communities in the New York Metro area cannot be missed. Thus, news of his sudden and massive cardiac arrest and subsequent clinical death sent shock waves through many of these communities. Many prayed and hoped for divine intervention. It happened. Reminiscent of the case of Lazarus, "this sickness is (was) not to end in death, but for the glory of God, so that the Son of God may be glorified by it" (John 11:4). Many things worked together in his favor. He was resuscitated and restored to life. Today, he lives without any major physical disabilities. Incredible! Personally, it is always a joy to see him, talk and pray with him. That he lives to tell his story is itself a miracle.

Parts of this story have been told through the "grapevines" and by friends and family. What this book seeks to do is to give a fuller account from "the horse's own mouth". In addition to providing the reader with the true "inside story" and "eyewitness" accounts, the book also leads us to think critically about the brevity and frailty of our lives, about the interaction between our physical and spiritual lives and about God's love and mercy. It even provides some insights into Ghanaian culture, history and politics.

Miracles have always been a difficult concept for some, particularly the non-religious and secular-minded, to understand or accept. The skepticism towards miracles associated with the rise of the scientific world view of the 17th century and even Protestant Reformers a century earlier still lingers on in different forms. While some perceive miracles as simply "scientifically" impossible, others consider them as mere luck or happenstance.

For G. Ofori Anor, miracles are "for real". While he cannot fully account for their existence, nature and purpose, he has seen them; experienced them, and will testify about them! In his testimony, he reminds all that there is a power beyond our human selves – the power of God capable and willing to change hopeless situations into hopeful ones.

While we read this delightful and inspiring story of redemption, let us give thanks to God for the life of the author and all who have seen miracles in their lives.

New Jersey

INTRO

Had I been the cat with nine lives, I probably would have used them all or getting close to using them all up. And if I were only human with one life to live like everyone else, I would be gone by now. I must fall somewhere in between, because I am still here, not exactly worried about how many lives I have left. Why worry about that over which you have no control? If ever I worry, it is about unanswered queries relating to who and what keep throwing chance after chance my way when most people do not get second chances in identical circumstances.

This is not a story of my entire life. Neither have I written a chronicle of notable achievements and excitable adventures of a great human figure in history. I have no such credentials as would enable me to write a classical autobiography.

Mine is simply a non-fictional pamphlet, maybe a journal, a testimonial narration of events in my life that I believe to be indicative of the presence *an unseen hand* -- the hand of a God, a Guardian Angel or an Ancestral Spirit -- in changing what should be the normal outcome of events. I most definitely have been the beneficiary of this presence in more ways than one. My gratitude runs into eternity.

What you are about to read are truthful recollection of notes tucked away in my memory, notes of things said, done, seen, touched or told. Some are from family records -- written or transmitted orally. If you find the narrative to be too true to be true, it is. That's what miracles are made of.

I nearly choked when my mother first introduced me to solid food. I wouldn't drown when, only a crawling infant, I fell into a well full of water. Neither did the wheels of a bus crush my skull as I laid underneath it. A ceiling fan broke and fell exactly where I sat seconds prior. What landed me unscathed on grass knoll rather than the ground floor concrete when I was literally flung from a third-floor verandah? I visited a friend whilst on vacation and found a job that made me a star. Have I not been granted reprieve even when I did egregious wrongs to my fellow man? You bet I have! A bunch of vigilante night prowlers missed me when they came to exact revenge. An encounter with deadly cold on a country road in New Jersey didn't terminate my life either. Then I survived a massive cardiac arrest that, instead of making me into a vegetable or a statistical number as it normally does to many a victim, made me into the "miracle man" that many see in me today.

How else could these be explained -- chance coincidences, miracles, lucky dips or what? Unable to extend my understanding beyond the limits of my intellectual insights and training, I have employed faith to explain the inexplicable to create a comfort zone within which I could operate. Perhaps a simpleton's way of explaining the inexplicable, admitting the inadmissible, and conceding to the inconceivable. But isn't that what Jesus meant when he said you can only enter the kingdom (of grace and peace) with a simple mindedness of a child?

I have had to tell and re-tell "my miracle" story to groups and to individuals. I have given testimonies in churches and in auditoriums. As it is with oral narratives, the chances for omissions, exaggerations and insertion of half-truths and inaccuracies are very real as you on telling them. So, I wrote to reduce those chances. And I have been helped tremendously by the accounts of my wife Florence, son Koby, daughters Asabea and Bedua and dear friend Dr. Kofi Adu. They told me most of what I have said and written about events on that fateful Tuesday, for, they were my eyes when I couldn't see, my ears when I couldn't hear, my mouth when I couldn't talk and my consciousness when I laid clinically dead. Their capacity to accommodate my annoying demands both during, after and unto this day is amazing. I cannot thank them well enough. I can only continue to love them unconditionally, as I always have, and for the rest of my life.

Mr. Clemente Lopes, principal of the intermediate school in Astoria, Queens where I fell and died clinically, filled me in completely and honestly with everything that happened there. Him knowing what to do and doing it with such authority and precision set the critical basis upon which my survival rested. To him and his assistant Alfredo ("Crazy" Alfredo), who literally commandeered an ambulance to administer critical first aid, I owe my survival, eternal gratitude and thanks. Is there any better way to capture Alfredo's gutsy character than describing him as "crazy"? Thank goodness for him being all that and more.

Whatever petty but important details left were supplied by my very dear friends (I call them "First Responders" - Sandy Atta Amoyaw, Albert Mensah, Retired Colonel Prince Twumasi-Ankrah, Dr George Lamptey), doctors, nurses and colleagues at my former workplace. They, especially the "First Responders" gave greater love than is common and are deeply appreciated.

I have done the little I could to provide information on some cultural practices found in Ghana, especially among the Akans. It is to help ease the uninitiated into some of the events herein.

Where I felt adequate, I commented on the world order and human condition in general as well as African/Ghanaian history and politics in particular. I took a few swipes at them. When you find them, please remember they are mine and mine only. Analyze, condemn, agree, disagree or ignore them as you choose. But please deny me not the right to express myself.

I am gratefully proud of my girls Asabea and Bedua who read portions of the draft and offered pertinent corrections and suggestions on language and usage. Their tremendous reading and writing talents shine in these pages.

New York

1

Yaa Asabea's Baby Last

Yaa Asabea - that's my mother. *Kaakyire* (pronounced *car-chi-rey*) is an *Akan* title assigned me that identifies me to be the last child in a sibling pool of five brothers and two sisters that she mothered in the over forty years that she stayed married to my father. My unique placement in the pool came with privileges and pain. One perk I remember and enjoyed the most was sitting on my dad's lap and enjoying a slice of meat from his plate slipped tenderly into my mouth while my brothers and sisters fought over whatever piece served them. I paid for this with beatings I took anytime mom and dad were not around to stop anyone.

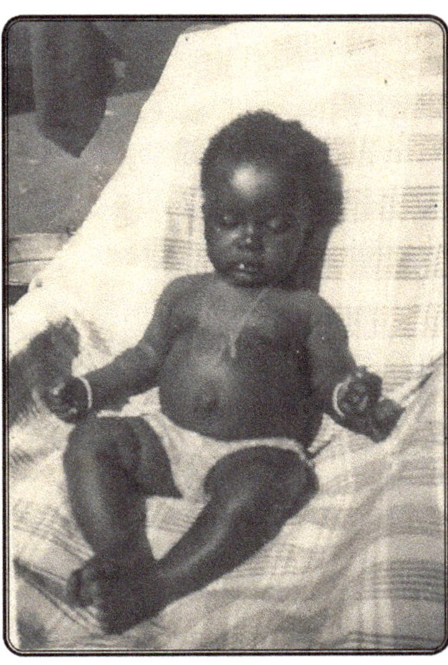

Yaa Asabea's Baby Last - 1950

Kwame is one of my other names. It is the name I came with, given me by the One who made me, my Creator. It is supposed to connect me to the day that my soul took leave of the Creator and began the trip into this earthly world of wealth and woes. My people, the Akans, say it is my **soul name** and it is the name by which I am known by whoever in the where-ever I came from. It is a fundamental belief held by the Akans of Ghana, the tribe into which I was born that your day name connects you to a spiritual origination. Thus once a week, four times monthly and fifty-two times yearly you stay reminded of the fact that there is a spiritual component within your human existence. My people have always held the human body to be a repository (a temple, if you would) of a spirit requiring that one stayed tuned to that spirit. Day names supposedly helped one do this on a daily, weekly, monthly and yearly basis. Akan soul or day names are (boys/girls): Sunday – *Kwasi/Akosua;* Monday – *Kwadjo/Adjoa;* Tuesday – *Kwabena/Abena;* Wednesday – *Kwaku/Akua;* Thursday – *Yaw/Yaa;* Friday – *Kofi/Afua;* Saturday – *Kwame/Ama.*

I have other names: *Naana Asoun Gaddiel Ofori Adjetewa Anor.* The first, *Naana,* is the female version of the reverential title *Nana* used to address royalty and wise accomplished senior citizens. I am unable to explain why I came to be given a girl's version because at no point in my life has there been anything girlish about me. Was there?

Asoun (numeral Seven) identified me as the seventh child of my parents.

Gaddiel is as European as Toyota is Japanese. Could it be English, Scottish, German etc.? I am unable to tell which European because I do not know. What I know is that my father, like many an African who accepted Christianity have been brainwashed into believing that "Christian" and European were one and the same things. Finding the African to be very spiritual, the European understood how he could use religion to get to the inner core of his being. They would employ religious subtleties to demonize and destroy African cultural practices at the core of their personal functioning and social organization. The resulting void would deftly be filled with European jibs and jibes.

Coming from a background of endemic treachery and greed, they couldn't belief the naivety and simple-mindedness of the natives they encountered. The European figured out quickly that a detribalized, "civilized" African is easier to colonize, dominate and made complicit in his own destruction than a fiercely "uncivilized" tribal native. A speech alleged to have been made on February 18, 1835 to the British parliament by a Lord Macauley maybe provides a fitting summary. *"I have travelled across the length and breadth of Africa and I have not seen one person who is a beggar, who is a thief. Such wealth I have seen in this country, such high moral values, people of such caliber, that I do not think we would ever conquer this country, unless we break the very backbone of this nation, which is her spiritual and cultural heritage, and therefore, I propose that we replace her old and ancient education system, her culture, for if the Africans think that all that is foreign and English is good and greater than their own, they will lose their self-esteem, their native culture and they will become what we want them, a truly dominated nation".*

Through religion will Africans become "civilized" and Christianity will be the religion of choice. By it, the African will be made to accept and internalize all manner of European cultural practices. Subsequently European names, marriage customs, languages, even food would become synonymous with "Christianity". Converts into the Christian faith were required to cement their faith by assuming European names deceptively tagged "Christian" names as their first names. If you knew not what to adopt, you were given one. Traditional and more meaningful soulful local names such as Abroampa, Okunka, Ntiwaa, etc. became satanic and were completely abandoned for all manner of European doggish tags some of them as meaningless as Carl, Stan, Donald, Rosaline or Betsy.

My father took or was given "Gideon". At least that is biblical in origin and might be construed to be Christian.

But *"Gaddiel"*? What was that? In college, I attempted to drop it for the more soulful Kwame. My father promptly threatened to disown me if I did. It's been stuck on me like ticks on a dog ever since.

My *Ofori* name was given me in honor of my long-gone illustrious ancestress, *Nana Afua Kyenkuwa Oforiwa*. In my tribal world, only the glorious departed had babies named after them. It is done in the hope that those qualities that made them so successful would rub off the newcomers. Combined with its appellation *Amanfo,* this name connotes loosely with *man or woman of the people.*

Anor is my father's surname. European traditions again have a lot to do with us assuming our father's last names and calling them sur/ family names.

Adjetewa comes with a long and intriguing story that needs recounting here and now. According to my mom, *Yaa Asabea,* I was conceived un-immaculately of human sperm and egg in Asante* Mampong in the house of this stoic Ashanti nobleman, *Nana Yaw Adjetewa.* Asante Mampong is a major metropolis within the historically famous and once mighty Asante Empire that the British destroyed on their way to making colonies and subjects of people who had graciously and unconditionally received and harbored them as they scuttled around the world looking for other people's resources to grab forcibly and pay nothing for them. There are words for that kind of behavior -- bullying and or stealing. Somehow, it has come to be deftly written and accepted into human consciousness as colonization.

Being the seventh and last in a sibling pool of five boys and two girls, I proudly wear the title **Yaa Asabea Kaakyire** (*Yaa Asabea's Baby Last*). I will, even unto death, remain the pampered, spoiled (and loathed by my siblings) knee child of the family. My late mother and father whom I recall with fond memories and gratitude were both native *Akwapims* (a subgroup of the Akan* ethnic stock) from the ancient village of Obosomase, tucked in the gorgeous mountain-valley, valley-mountain tapestry that must have been painted by the master artist himself -- Creator of the universe. Crudely interpreted, Obosomase means, "the realm of stone worshippers". It practically gave the simple-minded-nature- loving natives of this classic African village the inglorious classification of worshippers of stone gods and deities, which by Europeans definitions, meant their religion was animistic and satanic.   This woefully inaccurate description forgot to say that Obosomase was actually the spiritual capital of the Akwapims in much the same way as Christians and Muslims see Jerusalem and Mecca respectively as their spiritual holy lands. My father had gone to school to become one of the emerging scholar elite *(akrakyefo)* primed to assist Europe "Christianize, Commercialize and Civilize" Africa. That was how Europe would "heal" Africa, that the sixteenth century British explorer David Livingston myopically described as the world's "open sore".

My mother and five siblings were in Asante Mampong attached to my father's tailcoat, having been himself brought there as the District Health Inspector in the pre-independence colonial administration. Identified by an earth-brown helmet and a long ladle for scooping the bottom of barrels, they were the feared and despised "Town Council" officers who went from house to house, street to street, *chop bar* to *chop bar*, market to market to physically inspect and certify that all food, water, living quarters, etc. meet certain basic health standards. They inspected anything from water containers (barrels), cooking utensils, sleeping mats, mattresses, slaughtered animals, smoked fish, anything that had anything that humans consumed.

Looking back and at the abysmal failure of successive African-led post-independence administrations to deliver health and wellness services to the people, the colonialists deserve some modicum of applause even as we condemn and crucify them for other crimes committed against our humanity.

Mother and father occupied an apartment in this huge mansion owned by *Nana Yaw Adjetewa* who also lived-in other parts with his sister *Mame Afia Kani*. She waited on him hand and foot, catering to his daily living needs. My mother described *Mame Afia Kani* as a feisty no-nonsense middle-aged woman who was totally and unquestionably devoted to fighting for and protecting **all** her brother's interests. She was as unapologetically dedicated and committed to her brother probably as the legendary *Yaa Asantewa* was to Asante hegemonic interests.

Her feistiness, a bunch of missing teeth, age related physical ailments coupled with her unmarried (probably widower) status earned her the designation of a witch -- one who underwent mysterious transformations at night to do demonic evil to whoever she chooses. It was not uncommon for anyone, particularly women who carried these physical attributes to be called witches. As if dealing with the physical and emotional pains and pangs of old age were not enough, these old folks, even onto modern times wrongfully and egregiously abused, vilified, ostracized, tortured and sometimes lynched for being agents of the devil. They are insulted, called names, avoided, abused and refused by family, acquaintances and even strangers. They have no friends. Children are taught to stay away from them else evil will follow them all the days of their lives.

Many an accused witch coped with the situation by retreating from society into a self-imposed confined existence. In their misery, they build an invisible cocoon round themselves just so they can escape the taunts and insults, openly and insinuated, of a woefully superstitious and uninformed people.

Not *Mame Kani*. She fought back with fiery resistance and despised all those who in one swoop accused and condemned her. If anything, she assumed a more aggressive posture that made all fear her some more. She scared the daylights out of everyone. No one dared get on her wrong side for fear of what she might do to them when she traversed her "devil" kingdom at night fall. You better not cross her in the daytime for fear of what she might wrought when darkness came. Her reputation as a witch grew far and wide. She did not go out of her way to change anyone's mind. She grew stronger in her defiance. There can be no doubt that in her superior mind and spirit, she pitied the clueless humanity around her.

It was right under her nose, in the very house she lived with her brother that "un-immaculate" conception of me occurred. She declared openly that whatever came out of my mother's womb must be dedicated to the *Adjetewa* family, if the parents had any hope of returning to their Akuapem hometown with their baby trophy! Her asking price: a girl child to be named *Kani* after her good self while a boy child would be called *Adjetewa* after her brother. Call it what you may -- a demand, threat or warning. Everyone, including mom and dad, understood what she meant. And they took her seriously.

When I was born and taken home, she demanded to see the birth certificate. It had what she wanted: *Child's Name: Nana Kwame Adjetewa; Date of Birth: February 18, 1950; Father's Name: Gideon Kwaku Anor; Mother's Name: Felicia Yaa Asabea Djan: Place of Birth: Mampong Government Hospital.*

This is how I became the "son" of Nana Adjetewa of Asante Mampong. I did get to meet the man I was named after years later when I returned to Asante Mampong as a student learning the noble art of teaching at the University of Cape Coast. Partial requirements for the degree included two tours duty of student teaching at second cycle institutions of one's choice.

My second tour took me to Saint Monica's Teacher Training College in this town of my birth. *Mame Kani* was long gone to ancestral world. Nana Yaw Adjetewa was still alive and well advanced in age, an octogenarian. Even at that age, he stood tall and stately. His physical presence and the superiority of his character were undeniable. He towered over everyone like a colossus under whose feet all strode. When he rose to embrace me, I stood and stretched. I guess I was trying to be tall and graceful like him.

The Akans: This is an ethno-linguistic *group of people that can be found in the southern regions of modern day nations of Ghana the* Ivory Coast *in* West Africa. *They constitute the largest* ethno-linguistic *group in both countries and have a population of roughly 20 million people. They speak the* Akan language *of which Twi–Fante) constitute the main dialect. Subgroups of the Akan are identified by the dialectical version of the Akan language they speak, namely* Asante, Akuapem *and* Akyem, *Kwahu (together known as Twi), dialects are together known as Twi),* Agona, *Bor-Bor Mfantse, Abora, Gomoa (all of the Fante bloc). There is also the Bono subgroup that resides mainly in Ivory Coast and includes the Anomabo, Abura, Gomua) and* Bono. *The dialects are closely related. Subgroups of the Bia-speaking groups include: the* Anyin, Baoulé, Chakosi *(Anufo),* Sefwi, Nzema, Ahanta *and Guan. The Akan subgroups have cultural attributes in common, notably the origins, religion, political organization inheritance of property, and succession to high political office.*

2

The Water Well

I heard about my first tussle with death when I visited the place of my birth during a student teaching stint at Saint Monica's Teacher Training College in Asante Mampong.

I am in the third and final year of a course of study and training at the university to become a certified graduate teacher. One requirement for certification was an eight weeks internship of supervised teaching at any qualifying institution of one's choice virtually in any part of the country. I choose this Saint Monica's place for two reasons: it was renowned and prestigious and will look good on one's resume; secondly, I would be going back home to my place of birth, a homecoming of sorts.

The huge mansion still stood stately and imposing like the Acropolis of ancient Rome. I went one Saturday, hoping to run into anyone with any knowledge of the events of my birth twenty-two years prior.

Mame Afia Kani was long gone to the ancestral world. The old man was still there, very advanced in age. So also was another woman who had been there and remembered stuff.

On a prompt, I introduced myself and stated my mission thus:

" Nana, I have come back to the place where my mother tells me my umbilical cord was cut and buried and, if possible, to meet the man whose name I bear".

I went on to talk about my birth and parentage as my mother had told me.

Stone silence consumed the room and everything therein. All sat quietly as we waited for Nana Yaw Adjetewa to speak. You could tell the old man was struggling with his memory.

Then the old woman seated to my left softly but emphatically blurted out: "Ahaa, isn't it the boy child who nearly drowned in the well?"

Slowly but surely the old man's memory got the jolt it needed for things to seep back into consciousness. I stayed on for about an hour during which time we told everything he wanted to know about my family and our fortunes since we have been gone. It ended with Nana invoking ancient Akan blessings on me and praying for success to attend my life and way.

I left very satisfied and fulfilled.

I wanted to know a little more about the drowning. But the old woman was not all that forthcoming. She waved me off with the words: "O, its nothing. Just that you once nearly crawled into the water well in this very compound. You nearly died".

You know how our old folks can sound sometimes – dry and detached, especially if they do not intend to go any further with the discussion.

I realized it wasn't the right time and place to probe any further. I would take it up with my mother.

And that was exactly what I did when I returned home after completing the teaching assignment.

It took some doing to pry the details from my mother. She did not want to re-live an experience that traumatized both her and my big sister so badly.

I must have been no more than three years old when I nearly drowned – the first of my escapes from the grip of death.

The residents called it a well and it served all the folks who lived around it. It really was a huge tank that had been sunk into the ground. It was connected to several gutters that lined the edges of the roof of the huge building. These gutters collected rainwater and drained them into the tank making it into an extremely crucial reservoir of clean water for the folks who lived in the neighborhood. A round wall had been built around the opening over which a metal cover was hinged that enabled it to be locked for both security and safety reasons. Since it had not built with children in mind, no one realized that it was within crawling or hopping distance for troublesome and mischievous toddlers like me. Closed or opened children were never allowed anywhere near the well. Even fully-grown adults treaded with extreme caution any time they went by, especially when the top is opened. The reality of drowning accidents was always on everybody's mind.

This day, my sister Akua Kane, then a teenager and now deceased, had gone to the well to draw water. Unbeknown to her, I had slipped into the area carry nothing more than a "Milo" container which could hold no more than thirty-two ounces of water. What could that be used for in a household of two grown adults and six kids of varying ages?

The next thing she saw was me dangling on the edge of the noticeably short round wall that held the cover. She must have reached out to grab me. She missed and I tumbled over and fell into the tank. I tumbled down as would a piece of meat in a boiling soup. I was drowning! She held onto the short wall and swung her other hand back and forth in the still water as one does when feeling the way in the dark, all the while screaming and crying for help. Somehow by the inconceivable twist of chances (or luck) she caught me by the foot and yanked me out of the well. She flunked me to the ground, still screaming for help. I laid there limp and motionless for what must have been eternity.

Then I coughed and water gushed out of my tiny mouth and nose. A collective yell of relief and gratitude burst out from the small crowd that had by now formed. It was mainly women and young children not old enough to go to school. It being mid-morning, the men folk were out tending their farms or at work in government offices.

My mother caught the most hell imaginable from Mame Kani. She took some old-fashioned adult tongue lashing for child neglect and incompetent housewifery.

"I haven't forgotten Mame Kani waving her wrinkled index finger in my face and yelling like the witch she was: *'let me tell you something, if you allow something to hurt this boy, you and I will have a major problem because it will bother me big time'*". That was my mother quoting the "old witch" twenty-two years after the fact.

My sister, the poor girl, was served a good dose of insults and beating for something she didn't cause. Did she make me follow her?

Did she place me on the wall? Did she deliberately throw me into the well? What about a little love for being the one who ultimately pulled me out of the well? No thanks!! But that is the nature of things for children in adult-run African world. A child is always wrong until proven right! Meanwhile he or she is not given a chance to state a case or defend themselves. Never heard of child advocacy in traditional Africa. Thanks to European influence, much has changed. Much remains to be done.

A significant number of children in Africa eat only after the men in the family have gouged themselves silly of the best parts of the meal that contain nature's proteins, vitamins and essential oils needed for healthy growth. Children endure harsh punishments based on evidence whose validity and accuracy derives from nothing more than what an adult says.

I was once flogged and humiliated before the entire student body of the middle school I attended in Cape Coast -- Mensah Sarbah Middle School. I was found guilty and condemned on the words of a teacher who took fees from me but denied ever taking anything from me. No amount of protestation would make my father and the other teachers who served as prosecutors, judges and executors believe anything I said. They just won't listen. Never in my life had been truthful. Where, when and how the teacher character received the two shiny coins (two shillings each) is still engraved in my mind even unto this day. I still see him dropping them in the breast pocket of the white short sleeved shirt he wore over blue as mandated by his employers, the Ministry of Education.

I became the super rotten little demon who wanted to destroy poor Teacher Ngeza (that was his name) by falsely blaming him for school fees that I had stolen and misused. Nothing could be further from the truth. I gave that dishonest teacher four shillings (two shinny coins, two shillings each) that he probably spent on beer. I did my time in the physical pain and emotional humiliation that comes with being stretched and restrained hand and foot by four boys and given twelve lashes of the whip before the entire school body of teachers and students. The ultimate humiliation!

My justifiable and righteous indignation and revulsion for this man is unlike any that I would ever carry for any other person.

3

The Stump in the Road – Asante Mampong

Growing up in a society that forbade children addressing adults by their names meant we had to find appropriate titles for fathers. Back then. *Agya, Papa or Paapa* were the common currency fathers came in. We called ours Paapa, rarely Papa Anor which was his real name.

Back then, the doggish *Daddy or Da* for fathers and *Mom or Mommy* for fathers and mothers were virtually unknown. It was only the children of the nouveau riche city dwellers who called their parents Mommy and Daddy. Their parents, particularly the fathers, had stepped into the top administrative positions hitherto occupied by European colonists. They included top public servant, high ranking soldiers and policemen, college lecturers, bank officers, businessmen, politicians etc. They went on to assume all the trappings and perks that came with those positions. New and ridiculous ones were created and added. So also were new terms, concepts , vocabularies, etc.

One of them was the *"Dada Ba" (Daddy's Kid).* A *Dada Ba* was typically enrolled in an "international school", driven to and from school every day, lived in a household of maid servants, a "watchman" (security guard), garden boys, "driver" (chauffeur). He or she routinely went on trips to European destinations during the summer long vacation period.

International schools had emerged as the newest craze in newly independent Ghanaian education. They were privately owned and "privately" funded. They were elitists institutions where everything from furniture to stationary to snacks were of "international" quality.

Everything about them made a mockery of what obtained in public schools -- uniforms, transportation, teachers, buildings, etc. Their graduates ended up in equally elitist secondary schools such as Achimota, Mfantsipim, Wesley Girls High School etc.

Ghana's first president Kwame Nkrumah, attempted to counter the emergence of an elitist, exploitative self-serving leadership class with mass fee-free public education at all levels. Unfortunately, with his attention focused on myriads of continental and international affairs, he lost track of local saboteurs in his back yard. They were unwilling to let go of their dubious status, wealth and power and fought him every step of the way, some openly, some clandestinely. Some sold their loyalties to foreign interest for pittance. They corralled the system to preserve and consolidate their selfish and parochial interests. They, who were needed to help guide the newly independent nation into a viable political and economic entity with freedom, justice and fairness for all, drove Ghana on the highway to economic ruin and political instability through corruption and blatant thievery of communal wealth. While the father, Dada or Daddy, plundered state resources, the child, *"Dada ba"* (Dada's kid) proudly showed off imitations of European cultural practices acquired in elitist schools and overseas vacations at public expense.

These days, any man with balls strong enough to produce matured sperms and any woman whose eggs can fertilize and incubate them for nine months is a *Da* or a *Ma.*

I was no "Dada Ba" by the stretch of any definition. I came from that side (the huddled mass) where your father was just a *Papa, Paapa or Agya.* Mine was Paapa. He took up a job with Ghana's Ministry of Education right around the period of independence. The visionary Kwame Nkrumah, perceiving the need for skilled technicians to run the wheels of the massive industrial development he had in mind, had embarked on a massive expansion of educational opportunities for all. This of course was part of his drive to proof to the world, particularly those western ill-wishers that an educated African was "capable of managing his own affairs". Later developments on the continent would ironically proof that the African, everywhere from the dizzying heights of the Atlas Mountains in the north to tip of the Cape of Good Hope in the south is extremely capable of mismanaging his own affairs.

Nkrumah dreamt of an educated Ghanaian populace taking the lead in this huge undertaking on behalf of Africa much of which was still welting under the yoke of colonialism. Hence his universal free education for all programs.

My Paapa had earned his technical education credentials at one of the very few "Trades" school established by the British colonialist -- the Kibi Government Trade School. His trade was building technology, specifically masonry. He thus became a teacher of masonry at Asuansi Technical Institute near Cape Coast.

I remember Asuansi to be the place my early life began. I have fond memories of the place. Established together with the Agricultural Research Center nearly a century ago again by the British, it was a paradise in the jungle -- a very well laid out campus with fine buildings, well-tended lawns and gardens, a huge orchard belonging to the Agricultural Research Station, sports fields and lush greenery all around. We had electricity; pipe borne water even that far back. I began schooling at the local authority elementary school in the nearest village **Nyamedom** where Mr. Bruce was my first-grade teacher. His name is ingrained in my mind because he was such a wonderful human being.

I was in third grade when we were sent packing to Mampong Technical Institute, the town of my birth eight years earlier when Paapa was in the employ of the health ministry. This was in 1958. This second time around would not be a charm. Father would encounter circumstances that would alter the trajectory of his life and all of his family forever. It all began by him unjustifiably becoming the object of envy and hatred of a colleague instructor, a specimen of those humans who, unwilling and unable to succeed in their life's pursuits hold others responsible. He detested the pace at which Paapa grew and progressed on the job.

You see, Paapa, was a very mild-mannered six plus feet tall intellectually gifted man. I could swear that his IQ must have been significant positive deviations from the average. He, among things, had this uncanny ability to become functionally literate in any language after extremely limited exposure.

He was a devout Christian who endeavored to live by the dictates of the Presbyterian church. You could hold his picture up as the poster image of the proverbial *"Akuapem respect"* -- very devout Presbyterian, shy, soft-spoken, kind (to a fault) and as said earlier, highly intelligent.

His envious colleague allegedly employed a spiritual medium to "destroy" my Paapa. How can this be explained for a non-African to understand?

Simply put, the belief even unto this day, is prevalent among most Africans that anyone with reason to hurt another individual could do so spiritually. The soul of the intended victim is "taken" to any of the several powerful gods or deities scattered all over the place and a spell cast to cause premature or mysterious death, physical illness, severe mental illness, loss of work/property. My father's people, that is, brothers and sisters, believe this to be what this colleague did to Paapa. I was too young to understand and form an opinion. Even unto this day, I do not know who or what to believe.

It all began about six months after we moved into our new living quarters on school campus. Paapa's hobby was hunting. He owned two guns, a single and a double barrel that he purchased from the expatriate principal of Asuansi Technical institute as he was returning to England after completing his tour of duty.

Whenever the weather would permit, he would hunt small game in the bushes around the school each evening after classes. He was returning home after one of his daily late afternoon hunting sorties when he saw from a distance of about three hundred meters, a tree stump perched in the middle of the main road linking Mampong and Nsuta.

"A tree stump in the middle of the main thoroughfare used non-stop by both vehicles and human traveling between two major towns in the area? That's strange and unusual", he thought to himself. He ventured to within a hundred meters just to make sure of what he was seeing. The stump got bigger as he came closer. His sixth sense told him to back away and retreat from this strange phenomenon. He came home by another route and never breathed a word about this to anyone, not even his wife -- my mother.

Two days passed and nothing happened. He thought nothing further of it until the dawn of the third or fourth day. A loud rumbling noise shook the house and the room where he slept with my mother.

"Feli", he screamed for mother in a guttural voice, "am being choked!" Feli was how Paapa called my mother, it being the shortened form of Felicia, a supposed "Christian name"

"Who, what? Somebody, help, help!" mother yelled. All she saw was her husband clutching his neck and thrashing about on the bed.

For nearly four minutes, Paapa was locked in a violent struggle against an invisible "creature" that was attempting to strangle him by the neck. Then it stopped as suddenly as it had started. The noise and commotion had woken the neighbors next door and as is typical of Africans, the man of the house came rushing intending to render any help that might be needed. It was later in the morning when things had simmered down that Paapa told about the stump in the road. Everyone who heard him knew it was a bad omen. Signs pointed to the casting of an evil spell, a voodoo curse and Paapa was about to go down real hard. Who, what and why would not be known and answered until after three years of major upheavals in his life and that of his family?

A week or so might have passed without any dramatic happenings. Then little by little Paapa's countenance and outward nature began to change. He became sullen and withdrawn. Of course, he had been made to give up hunting. He muttered words to himself and showed no interest in engaging anyone in a meaningful conversation. The once proud "British trained" scholar and gentleman now cared extraordinarily little about personal grooming and dressing.

By the third month, the tell-tale signs of acute depression and schizophrenia were evident. Incessant visits to conventional medical establishments did nothing to reverse the trend. Native doctors, herbalists and spiritualists that were consulted all agreed that Paapa had a *"non-hospital"* illness. None had a cure for it. He's been pummeled spiritually and would require treatment far beyond normal human capacities.

He started hearing voices that told him to hurt himself, worse still, commit suicide. Curtains, belts, clothesline, linens, clothes, furniture, name it became tools for self-destruction. Our house had to be stripped bare of virtually everything because everything became a tool for suicide. Round the clock observation and strong-arm tactics needed to be employed to foil incessant suicide attempts that included jumping off moving vehicles or lunging himself at approaching vehicles or hanging himself by door or window curtains. My mother a mere five-feet three inches, one-hundred-sixty pounds woman became the main caretaker. No one could explain how she garnered the physical and emotional strength that enabled her corral and subdue and contain the six foot plus monster that father had become.

I was eight. I have not, and probably will never be able to erase from memory the picture of dad chained to a pole in the main courtyard of Mampong police station. I stood there in tears as he violently thrashed himself about struggling to break free of the restraining chain.

A small crowd had gathered. Someone who apparently knew me pointed my way and said "Look, over there, that is his last born".

Then like a choir, on its conductor's prompt, a mournful moan went out: "Oooh!!"

The only consoling element of his violent outbursts was that they were directed at harming himself and no one else.

Shortly after, he was understandably relieved of his teaching job for health reasons. With dad in the hospital the order came for us, the family, to vacate the official staff bungalow. With that came the crushing down of our little sheltered world of relative comfort and privilege. We were neither rich nor affluent. He had just made it into the rungs of emerging middle-class comforts. Father, no doubt intended to move us further.

Now we would have to look elsewhere for survival.

4

Three Years in Hometown Obosomase

At eight years, I was too immature to understand the whys of what had befallen our family. Together with my brother Theo, Kwabena Opare (Theo), ten, and sister Ama Djanmea, (aka Emelia or Emy), twelve, we were sent to live out the next three years of our childhood in the old village Obosomase under the care of our now deceased maternal aunt, Aunt Kwabea. How we came out of there must have been by the special mercies of the good Lord. I also assign some credit to the unseen support of those gone before us into the spiritual world of the ancestors.

Paapa's side of the family would have nothing to do with us. His three brothers and two sisters rejected us more because of their own financial inadequacies than it was for any ill will they had for their brother and his family.

With no one to pay his school fees, my big brother Kwabena Amoah (aka Gideon), seventeen or eighteen, dropped out of junior college to go work. My other teenage sister Akua Jane, fifteen, also dropped out of high school to assist mother take care of the stricken father. At that young age Gideon was already a rising star, an accomplished piano player and a gifted athlete who ran the field and played tennis for the school. Akua Jane was on target to enroll in high school the following academic year. Instead, she joined mother traveling all over Ghana desperately seeking treatment for father.

Mother's determination to stay true to her marriage vows, saw her by dad's side every single day as he is moved from facility to facility all over Ghana in search of a cure for a sickness which had by now been diagnosed to contain deep spiritual prognosis. It was not a "hospital illness" for which any known treatment was readily available. It had deep spiritual antecedents and needed to be treated as such.

The three of us children went overnight from sleeping in beds to squirming on floor mats patrolled by black ants whose bites stung like a thousand pin pricks. Balancing a bucket on the head and trekking through the wet dawn brush to draw water from the river wrapped in a two-yard strip of cloth in one of the coldest places in Ghana was torture for anyone, especially an uninitiated nine-year old. You needed to learn overnight to tell the difference between helpful plants and harmful ones like poison ivy to avoid them. Survival in the new and unfamiliar environment for us "three babies" was rough and tough. We had to adapt and adjust fast or perish.

As quickly as our world has been turned upside down, we had to learn how to handle a cutlass or a hoe to weed, till the soil, plant seeds, fetch firewood, dig yam mounds etc. The clothes that we had on our backs as we exited Mampong remained all that we had for three years. My aunt gave of her best but providing for three additions to her own three children was not an easy proposition. Breakfast, lunch and dinner were compressed into one meal with a "eat what comes" tag.

Obosomase is a small village in the back country. It is set in a very lush tropical forest. Nature provides much valuable sustenance through an endless supply of plants and animals which required little or no technology to gather and consume. If you knew where to look, you could enjoy a good meal anytime made up of mushrooms, avocado, spinach, wild yams or cassava, snails washed down in uncontaminated rainwater. But you had to know where to look!

I lost little of the smarts, sense of humor, fun loving, extroverted personality that I had been endowed with and remained the ingeniously mischievous little rascal that I was during the happy days of Asuansi and Mampong. I pinched a penny here, a penny there, did graffiti and told tall tales.

I found an accomplice in another rascal Adjei Danquah. Being the son of the resident Catechist of the Methodist Church, he was almost untouchable. This meant that I bore all the guilt and brunt of punishments anytime we got caught. For instance, the woman who once caught us scribbling obscenities about human male and female genitalia on a wall never saw my accomplice. I was assigned all the blame and punishment.

One very naughty episode had to do with me scheming to extort money from a couple of older relatives to pay the fare to see my father who I hadn't seen for two years. One day, we woke up to the information that Paapa had been brought to a faith healing camp in a town called Tinkon, about twenty kilometers drive away. I missed father so badly and was consumed by the urge to see him. How was I going to come up with two shillings to pay the fare for me and my brother to go see him? That was a lot of money at the time.

Without telling my brother, I went to one of our great grand aunties and concocted a tale.

"Nana, your sister Awo says she needs a quick loan of two shillings to buy something. She is out on the street and has no money on her. She says you will pay you back as soon as gets home"

Nana readily gave me two one shilling coins to be given to her elder sister out there on the street. I gleefully took the money ran to my brother and told a finder's keeper story. The trip never materialized because no driver would offer seats on their vehicles to two unaccompanied infants for a million shillings!

I do not remember what I did with the money. But for sure none of the two great grannies saw anything of it. The truth came out a couple of weeks later when I had completely forgotten all about it. When word got to my mother, she came by as soon as she could. She refunded what I had taken and apologized profusely for what I had done. You can imagine how embarrassed she was and the fury with which she laid unto the hide on my behind. For months my friends, peers and even adults subjected me to wicked name calling, insults and accusatory glances. Most adults saw me as a kid bound for a life of crime and notoriety if left unchecked.

By 1962, father had been cured of all that ailed him. It took a combination of western conventional medicine and traditional "home" medicine with all its spiritual supplements to get there. The doctors of hospitals played as much a role as Togbe Amuzu at his healing camp deep in the farmlands of Suhum in Ghana's eastern region.

He is re-hired and posted back to Mampong. After a year's probationary assignment, he is confirmed and sent over to Kpandu

Technical College. Three years after our hasty dispersal, the Anor family was reunited once again – father mother, five children.

When time came after almost three years to leave, I admittedly had no love for my home village. But infantile experiences are known to be fantasies that are as permanent as baby teeth. As years rolled by and life took me to other lands and through several adventures and experiences, I came to acquire great fondness for the place. My parents had a lot to do with this. Hailing as they were from there, they constantly reminded us of our duty to go back and help lift it up. Paapa declined to acquire landed property and settle permanently any place else other than the village. It is this emotional fondness and attachment that would have me maintain an ongoing desire to "give back" to my place of origin.

So in 1992/93, I made my first move towards giving back. The New York-New Jersey-Connecticut tri-state area that I lived was teaming with a sizeable number of Ghanaian immigrants with Obosomase origins. I knew this because I was a leading member of the community. I had gone on from being the General Secretary of the Okuapeman Fekuw to become the Deputy Secretary General of the National Council of Ghanaian Associations. So I knew. What started as courtesy phone calls to persons such as Dr Clarence, Cynthia, Helena, Emma, Eugene and others morphed into a movement, Obosomasefo USA, that was to finance a street lightning project in the village. I became the leader of this loose association. We each voluntarily doled out amounts ranging between $100 and $300 for a two-phased project. The first phase, a novelty on the Akuapem ridge, was completed and commissioned in 1993 and the historic town beamed in its lighted glory with phase two pending.

In the end, however, the circumstances of its commissioning would leave a feeling of bitterness and regret in me and all the rest whose gifts and donations went to fund the project. Reason: the then village chief and his elders somehow managed to assign credits to themselves, USAID, the national government and other characters that knew next to nothing about how it came to be. Obosomasefo USA, was denied a deserving courtesy of mention and recognition. Phase two would stay pending. The fire in me to give back was effectively quenched and would remain so for years to come.

5

Happy Days in Kpandu

The one year that we spent in Kpandu would be amongst the happiest in my early life. That town in the 1960s was arguably one of the most promising middle-income urban towns in Ghana. Renowned for creating national and international currency for ***"Borborbor"*** music and dance, Kpandu, fits in well with some similar towns where life was good -- Cape Coast, Obuasi, Swedru, Tamale, Oda, Nkawkaw, and a few others. They swung at a moderate pace somewhere between the fast lanes of the likes of Accra /Kumasi/Takoradi and the sleepy hollowness of the countryside. This was a time that one would describe as Ghana's "golden age" (considering the decadence and decay that were to consume the country in later years).

I would learn in later years as a student of history that Kpandu was a bastion of support for Dr Kwame Nkrumah and the Convention Peoples' Party. ***Borborbor,*** an electrifying recreational music and dance gave his independence and self-government message an infectious rhythm and fire that carried far and wide beyond the place of its origin.

There was this woman popularly known as "Ghana Girl". She was the lead singer of one group whose. Her name is lost from history's pages. She performed regularly with her group at official functions, soaked head to toe in the party's red, white and black colors, a most admired patriot and hero. What happened to her when Nkrumah's government was overthrown in 1966 is anybody's guess.

Kpandu was especially good, at least from the perspective of a ten-year-old boy in 1960. You felt safe and secured wherever you went. My peers mimicked the neighborliness of their parents by being themselves very friendly, funny, carefree and mischievous as children should. My Form One teacher at the then E.P. Boys Boarding School, Mr. Asamani, shares the honor of being the other half of my all-time favorite teachers. Mr. Bruce, my first-grade teacher, was the other half of my life's coin.

Could it be that I loved Kpandu this much because it was here that I had my very first crush on a girl? My boyish testosterones were beginning to fire and Patience (that's her name) caught my eye and fantasy. She was the prettiest girl I had ever seen! No one talked, walked, smiled or cried like her. Being classmates meant I saw her most of the school hours. The draw down on this was that I couldn't manage my emotions well enough to follow class rules. I talked too much, ran around too often, was too eager to help or do anything that would catch her attention. I doubt she ever noticed anything more than the annoying little pest that the teacher had to deal with.

I talked about her to anyone who would listen, but never had the courage to say hi to her, let alone tell her about my feelings. All I did was make silly infantile giggles and faces when I saw her or heard her name mentioned. I manufactured and told lies about moments we had together to my boy peers who were dumb enough to believe and couldn't muster any courage to verify the truth.

But we were pre-teens who dabbled in the naughty shenanigans that kids everywhere dabbled in. We were boys being wickedly mischievous, but genuinely without any evil intentions!

A girl joined our class sometime in the middle of the school year. We did not find her physically attractive. I fact, we all saw her as the ugliest girl on that side of the world. Boy, did we tease and molest her! We called her unflattering names, pulled her hair, and bullied her, all for no other reason other than that we thought she was ugly.

We yelled out her given name to molest her. She had a name that we found weird and unusual. I would learn in later years that the name she bore was an incredibly special one given only to children that were classified as "spiritually special".

You see, the belief is held, even unto this day among my people that mothers who continuously loose children at birth are in competition with another woman in the spirit world. This "spirit mother" loans out the babies for a brief period and hurriedly claims them back after they are born. Hence the revolving door of birth and instant death.

This would seem a very convenient explanation for seemingly insoluble phenomenon like infant mortality in primitive societies. You lived with many natural episodes like volcanic eruptions, floods by couching them in spiritualities.

Incidence of high infant mortality was dealt with in similar fashion. Babies were classified as *"kɔsanbra" (go-come-back)* babies by incidents of high infant mortality in some families. These kids are given weird names or physical marks (slight mutilations) just so they would not be recognized and claimed by the spirit mothers when they show up. That way their survival is assured.

She had a weird name and an equally weird scar on her face. The poor girl must have internalized all these for she kept to herself most of the time.

But boy was she tough! The heavens save you if she ever grasped you in her hands. You are sure to be given a beating that would last you a lifetime. She was tall, muscular and strong. Her kick was like that of a mule and her knuckles packed punches that felt like iron. I knew because she caught me once and gave me a never-to-be forgotten dose of her "who is our mama" walloping.

I screamed an unflattering name at her and took off, believing I could outrun her in an open field. I had made a wrong move. *Nutsu* (name shortened) could chase down a deer! She bore down on me like a raging bull and caught up with me in seconds. The dame gave me the whipping I probably deserved!

One of my fond memories of Kpandu had to do with how the Evangelical Presbyterian Middle School in which I was enrolled was administered. Each school day consisted of morning and afternoon sessions. All sessions Monday to Thursday as well as Friday morning were for academic work – Reading Writing, Arithmetic, Nature Studies, Geography, History, Hygiene, etc.

Friday afternoons were for sports and games. Every kid enrolled in the school – chronic truants included -- lived for those Friday afternoon hours between 1:30 and 4 o'clock. The draw of sports, especially soccer, was magnetic. Those two plus hours from books (and the whip) were priceless. Organized into teams, we played fierce competitive matches in soccer, volleyball, netball and *"ampe"* for girls for fun magnified many times over.

I played the position of goalkeeper for my team, Lucky Stars, whilst my brother Theo played the position of central defender right in front of me. We made an impregnable defensive duo! I haven't lost memory of some excitingly fierce battles with our main rivals, Mulpo Babies.

It probably is by no accident that it is in this sunshine town that I would enjoy one meal that still waters my pallets any time that I recall the experience. Even unto this day.

The day was a Saturday within the month of August. Schools were out for the long summer vacation. Big brother Kwabena Amoah (Gid), now deceased, then in his twenties, had returned home from the college in another part of the country where he was training to become a certified schoolteacher. Knowing full well that big brother could easily take charge of the household in their absence, father and mother decided to take a rare vacation trip back to grand old home village, about two hundred miles away. There was a reason why such trips were rare. The journey required traveling by motor vehicle on a long winding roadway through the treacherous Kpevie mountains in the Volta region of Ghana. Anyone who has endured that experience would understand why it was, in those days, a graveyard for many reckless drivers and hapless passengers.

With our parents gone, *'bra'* Amoah supervised our lives in much about the same way that our parents did. He ensured that myself, Opare (Theo) and Djanmea (Emy) stayed true and committed to performing our daily chores. He had control over what and when to eat. Thankfully, in addition to a very sharp and bountiful stock of intelligence, he was easy-going, fair minded and fun loving. Whereas fate made us siblings, life's experiences made him into my mentor, roll model and a friend in whom I am very well pleased even unto this day.

It therefore came as a surprise when this day he unilaterally issued a strange decree that there was going to be a single meal the entire day. It was going to be everyone's favorite -- *nkatekwan* (peanut butter soup) and rice. That was the sweet end, the bitter part being that there was going to be just one feeding time the entire twenty-four hours. How could anyone in their rightful mind expect forever-hungry boys of pre-teen years survive on a single meal a day? As if that wasn't bad enough, food was not going to be ready until mid or late afternoon. This part of the bad deal was dictated by the very demanding processes under which this most desired, super glorified *nkatekwan* was prepared, to wit, Roasting the nuts, separating, and removing the husks, pounding into a crunchy mass, grinding into a smooth creamy paste, liquefying with water, draining to remove undesired sediments, blending with spices and cooking. These processes together meant several hours of painstaking labor. Cooking on the coal pot took forever, it being a time when gas/electric ovens and stoves, microwaves and blenders were unknown.

But big brother insisted and supervised. Sister Djanmea complained but labored in the kitchen. I and Opare played and grumbled while our empty tummies rumbled. The aroma that poured out of the boiling soup made us hungrier and angrier. By three that afternoon, the battle was over. The soup featuring a bit of everything -- mushrooms, snail, *"wele"* (cow skin) etc. was ready. So was the rice. We sat down to a breakfast-lunch-dinner meal that truly remains the tastiest in my mind and on my tongue.

Good things they say never last long. So it was with those happy days in Kpandu. One year and it was all over. Father was sent packing. (they call it 'transfer') to a new assignment in Cape Coast, hundreds of miles on the other side of the country. As coat trailers, we were sent along as well.

I do not know whether the excitement of a long bus trip to the other side dulled out the painful reality of leaving what I thought was a great time in Kpandu. But soon Kpandu faded into memory only to creep back from time to time as sweet dreams.

6

Ogua, Cape Coast!!

The year was 1961. My parents brought me to this very cosmopolitan town as an eleven-year-old middle school form two pupil and I would permanently leave it in 1976, a fully grown and matured (hopefully) adult in possession of a bachelor's degree from the university that bore its name -- Cape Coast.

It was also in Cape Coast that I survived my second close encounter with death, the first being the near drowning incident when I was a toddler.

I had gone with a friend, Victor, to the house of girl for whom he had a serious crush. Comfort's (the girl's name) father was the general manager of the giant colonial multinational company UAC. They lived mightily in a massive mansion perched on a hill in a very exclusive part of the town. We travelled by public transportation, a "Municipal Bus". Lost in my own boyish thoughts about nothing in particular, I nearly missed my stop on the way back from disappointment and frustration. I rushed to the exit and attempted to get off just when the driver jerked the bus into motion. I was spurned around, flung, and thrown out of the bus like a rag doll. I landed under the chassis. The driver heard the screams of people around and driver braked just in time. My head laid no more than a couple of inches right next to one of the huge rear tires. The slightest movement of the wheel would have guaranteed my head being crushed and my brains mashed into mincemeat. I was pulled out with only few scratches on my elbows and knees. The bus and my friend continued on and I went my merry way. Had I died; it would have been for naught (foolish die!). We never saw the girl for whose sake I had gotten on the bus! She didn't even know we were hiding in the bushes around the bungalow in which she lived with her dad and family in an exclusive part of the town.

Much of my physical and emotional transformations occurred in Cape Coast. The fore skin on my penis was cut here by a traditional surgeon *"wanzam"* without the benefit of any pain numbing medication, before or after. I took the bitter rite of passage into manhood pill on an early weekday morning in the backyard of a mud house in the *Zongo* suburb. School had recessed for the long summer vacation. His son Baba who incidentally was my classmate, covered my eyes with his tiny hands as the knife ripped apart that loose hanging skin and left me bloodied in indescribable pain.

I was motivated to 'cut my penis' by events of the prior school year. Before Cape Coast, no one really cared about who was circumcised and who wasn't. Not once was it mentioned or made a condition for participation in any boy game or activity. Not in Cape Coast. The gods save you if caught uncircumcised. Like Rudolph the red-nose reindeer, you would be called names and refused participation in all kid games. The certification ritual was amazingly simple. The boys would form a circle around you at the playground and dare you pull down your shorts and "show it". Taking too long meant you were *"kɔte bɔtɔ"*, (uncircumcised) in which case they will tackle you to the ground and strip you naked. Then everyone, including the girls, will hear about your unclean condition. A life of ridicule and harassment is what awaits you – in school, on the playground, anywhere that two or three youngsters are gathered. The secret to avoiding all that was to keep to yourself and shun the boys and the playground as much as you could. But being an extrovert, I could not stay away. And they did not have to strip me down. I unwittingly and foolishly exposed myself. A peeking tom watched as I carelessly urinated in an open area. He saw the dangling foreskin. I caught enough hell time to make me swear never to return to school after the long vacation an uncircumcised brat.

By the end of August, the wound had healed nicely, and I was the proud owner of a hot dog size penis that I was dying to show off to the guys when schools re-opened in September.

But that was not to be. Having passed the Common Entrance examinations for admission into secondary school, I was shipped off to Accra to start off the next leg of formal education. I would spend the next three years of my life under the care of a family member and his wife while I attended Odorgonno Secondary School, better known for its acronym *O.S.S.A.* They became my guardians for three turbulent years.

OSSA was an all-boys day school with an envious record of having defeated Team Ghana in a soccer match in the late 1950's. Unfortunately, it was rather notoriously famous for a series riotous protest by the students over the sub-par education they were given. A typical case of the bad that men do living with and after them while the good is buried in steel encasement.

OSSA had just been absorbed into the public funded school system and put in the administrative care of a principal who had a nose for corrupt practices and incompetence. Like many public servants of the time (sadly even today), this man squandered the public charge that was entrusted to him on the altar of arrogance and corruption that bothered on thievery and sheer wickedness. He took money under the table and loaded sixty students into a classroom capped for thirty.

The greatest harm he did was in the area of pedagogy and instruction. He did not consider it important to hire qualified tutors to nurture the minds of the youngsters whose intellectual, social, and physical growth and development had been entrusted to him. He packed the staff with several mediocre personnel, underpaid them and allegedly pocketed the difference.

Subjects like French and Geography and the Physical Sciences were so poorly taught that we loathed them. Apart from a few American Peace Corp volunteers, there simply were no Math or Science teachers. For most of our early years, we sat in classrooms and waited for teachers to show up at their own leisure, if they did at all. The few times one was brought in for French, for instance, he would be a Togolese hustler who evidently could speak French but had little or no teaching expertise or experience. Then there was Geography. The man hired himself to teach it. Of course, he hardly ever showed up to teach. When he did, he rattled the names of rivers and mountains in South America to show off the fact that he had a college degree in the subject. I heard him more than once spew forth the words "Atacama, Cotopaxi, Orinocoo, Chimborazzo , Machu Pichu ......" I would find out in later years that they are all geographical landmarks on the South American continent! Poor twelve and thirteen-year olds! We sat there in awe and admiration of what we thought was intellectual brilliance! Those of us who went on from there to sixth form and then to universities did so by self-instruction (especially in the Arts), self-reliance and brutish hard work.

Needless to say, the school suffered years of fluctuating fortunes in infrastructural development and academic performances. Thankfully, successive administrations after this poor specimen of a public servant evidently did extremely well to change things. Today, my alma mater is housed in a sprawling campus complex and is listed among the top high schools in Ghana.

One fateful day in my third year, Ben, a classmate, and I ran from school way ahead of the two o'clock dismissal time. Unfortunately, we ran straight into this headmaster riding back to school in a taxi. We eluded capture and ran further away, or so we thought. Unbeknown to us, my face had been deposited solidly in his memory. Two weeks after our encounter, I went to him to counter sign a fifty pesewa (about four shillings or a dollar) money order my dad had sent me before it could be cashed. Back then, that was worth millions to a schoolboy!

He took the paper, signed and stamped it. Then he casually lifted the table pad, slotted it underneath and without looking at me calmly said: "go bring the other boy you were with so I can expel you both or you will go alone".

Oh! oh! Busted! I knew I was in huge trouble, trouble that could end in me being expelled, permanently thrown out of school.

"What are you saying, sir", feigning all the innocence I could.

"You know what I am saying", he yelled words spiced with some unsavory expletives in the local Ga language.

"Go bring that ruffian you were with or you will go home all by yourself. Get out now before I slap you!", he screamed my way.

In fact, I believe the only reason he let me go was because it was a late Friday afternoon and like everyone else, he was just about leaving for home. Had it been any other day or time, I am quite sure he would have had my backside whipped by one of his professionally bankrupt minions until I confessed.

Whipping by cane and other forms of corporal punishments were not exactly uncommon in the school at this time. And there was no shortage of enforcers. One particular character doubled also as the chief enforcer and a Math instructor of sorts. He excelled more at the latter than the job for which he was paid. He boasted openly and loudly about his ability to employ a cane to peel the skin off the backside of any human and not break a single sweat.

To us the poor students who suffered the abuse, we swore that he was a psychopath who enjoyed some form of orgasmic pleasure out of the pain he administered unto his victims.

Weeks passed and I did my best to hide from the headmaster. Luckily, our paths never crossed paths to the end of the school year. Just before we left for home, I wrote to my dad to cancel the postal order lying that I lost it. Dad sent back word that the post office said it had been cashed. Who cashed and pocketed the money?

Finding ways to survive and commute between Laterbiokoshie and Adabraka, Monday to Friday, to receive secondary education as a day attendee, consumed most of the three years that I lived with my new guardian. It took everything that my young energies could endure. It must have sucked the energies and resources of the guardian as well. Now grown and raising children my own, I am able to appreciate what he and his wife had to endure.

My guardian had a nickname given him by his contemporaries who thought of him as cut in the mold of legendary African freedom fighter Jomo Kenyatta who led the Mau Mau freedom fighters against British colonial rule in Kenya. European nations, in the 19th century had shamefully and unapologetically sliced up Africa amongst themselves as colonial possessions. They took possession of all human and material resources, appropriated and exploited them as they wished with accountability only unto themselves.

When African nationalists rose against this, the Europeans killed those they could (Lumumba, Sgt. Adjetey, Cpl. Attipoe, Amiclar Kabral and countless others in Kenya, the Congo, Namibia, South Africa etc.) and branded those they couldn't as monsters and psychopaths with demonic intentions to kill all Europeans and their loyalists. As if that could be done!!! Such was the fate of arch nationalists Kwame Nkrumah, Jomo Kenyatta, Sekou Touré, Nelson Mandela and others who survived. Tragically, many Africans internalized such mischaracterizations and saw their freedom fighter leaders as the Europeans wanted them to be seen -- evil, wicked troublemakers.

My guardian proved to be as mean spirited as advertised. Neglect and physical abuse characterized the relation between us. I was given little to eat, just enough change for a "tro-tro" ride to and from school each day. To get by, I would run errands for neighbors who would reward me with loose change or food to fill my ever-empty, pre-teen belly. My benefactors here included Kofi Maame, the porridge seller, Mama, Mamkpa, V.C Commey and his wife, Bob the taxi driver and others time has wiped from my memory. To them I owe a big chunk of my survival in those years.

My guardian needed the littlest of excuses to lay into my emotions and frail body with verbal abuses, body blows and kicks. His stay-home wife fanned the flame with long reports everyday he came home from work, reports that were spiced to incense even the angel that sat at the right hand of God Almighty. I lay no claim to having been the paradigm of an altar boy. But I was no more mischievous than a typical thirteen-year-old teenager.

He would not buy me new clothes. Other than my school uniforms which father sent from Cape Coast every now and then, I had two shorts, three shirts and an old pair of canvas shoes popularly known as 'cambuu". The shirts were all ones he had discarded because they were too old, had holes or stains. Of course, they were oversized and fitted me as they would fit a scarecrow on a corn field.

Consequently, I was driven to do what juveniles who felt emotionally and physically deprived do -- join a neighborhood street gang. "39 Steps" was the one I hooked up with. My pals included such characters with *tough guy names* (nick) names like King Percherper, Aturupepe, Ato Kukurudu, Sammy B, Gabby Hayes, B Santo, Oblatse, Paa Moore and his brother Action. The oldest and most vicious member, Paa Nii and his brother Teiko did not care for any nicknames.

I had two street names, "Shoto-Shoto" and "Drotse" (pronounced *drawcher*). The first came from the oversized hand down shirts that I wore. The boys teased me silly with the nickname "Shirty-Shirty" which over time became "Shoto-Shoto". They called me "Drotse" which in *Ga* language meant "lord of testicles" because they said they could tell from the way I walked that I had excessively big testicles dangling between my legs. No one could claim they ever saw my testicles anyway!

"39 Steps" was essentially a club of teenage kids who cut school to hang out to smoke cigarettes. Occasionally, we would steal foodstuffs from nearby farms. We did nothing overtly violent like burglary or terrorizing residents.

Over time I grew bigger and taller and would fight back anytime my brother-guardian attempted to "discipline" me. His concept of discipline was to physically assault me with his bare hands or the whip. One day he attempted to execute one of his usual violent assaults. It was an exceptionally violent attack. I fought him to a standstill, sustaining cuts and scratches on my neck and arms. I said what I thought of him in vile insults and curses. He threw me out of the house with the words "no sane person throws money at pigs". In other words, it was not worth the while to expend money on a hopelessly useless creature like me. I went back to my parents in Cape Coast. With evidence of physical abuse on my body, they at last came to believe what I had been telling all along that the man who was supposed to protect me was abusing me to death!

This marked a major turning point in my life. Father found a way to put me in the school's hostel which provided paid board and lodge for out-of-town students. Suddenly, I found myself in a controlled, structured environment with other youngsters who well fiercely determined to make something out of their lives. I was suddenly thrust into a culture of purpose and effort. I went overnight from an abused, troubled and drifting youngster to a determined, ambitious, competitive student. The traits that identified the students in the hostel rubbed off me as cream rubs off patched skin. I set academic goals -- to make it to the university. The harm that guardian thought he was doing me turned out to be my saving grace. I went on from there to Sixth Form at Winneba Secondary School and then to an honors program at Cape Coast University.

This man, my brother, harbored an intense anger at mom and dad over their disapproval of the girl he wanted to marry and married. Sister was her name. When they met, Sister was a pretty teenager, aged no more than 17. Though developed well beyond the averages of a tenth-grade schoolgirl, she legally speaking was still a minor. Big brother was hopelessly smitten the minute he laid eyes on her. He began dating her. She began to take liberties including skipping school and sleeping outside. Her father justifiably became incensed and set traps to catch the corrupting agent. The trail led to lover boy's home. Consequently, her father had him arrested and held in jail for harboring a runaway minor. It took a lot of doing by my parents and some elders to eventually settle things out of court. He was let go on the strict orders that he would stay away from the girl. Having been smitten by the love bug, he did not. Rather he made plans to marry her. Mom and dad were understandably upset and joined other elders to withhold their approval and blessings for marriage. They married, nonetheless. The couple, for inexplicable reasons, harbored intense anger and animosity for all naysayers, an emotional state that would linger for a long time. I would be the closest they could get to mom and dad in acting out their anger over their disapproval of the marriage.

I do not hold any grudges or bitterness over the many incidences of incidences of physical and emotional torture I suffered that nearly ruined my growth and development. I have matured to understand that I was caught in a strive of sorts between our old school parents and a love stricken son, my brother, who was hell bent on claiming his independence. Neither parent nor son understood the forces that were pulling them apart.

One adventure during this chapter of my life that I recall with nostalgic fondness consisted of a twenty-six mile foot walk from Obosomase to Accra by myself and my cousin Patrick who like me, was a high schooler. I was fourteen years old, to be precise. We had come to the village to participate in funeral celebrations for our late uncle. It didn't take too many days for our city-schooled teenage minds to become completely drenched in village-induced boredom. We craved for action. A foot hike to Accra, twenty-six miles away was what caught our fancy.

Early the next morning, we strapped bags that held our few belongings unto our skinny backs and hit the road. It took all of nearly ten hours of trek under a blazing August tropical sun. We walked as leisurely and relaxedly as we could, caring about nothing behind, beside or before us. When the sun's presence became too hot and unbearable, we took rest stops under tree shades. The sights consisted mostly of corn and cassava farmlands, uncultivated undergrowth, chirping birds rummaging for foods in treetops or simply sheltering from the hot sun. Occasionally, a vehicle would speed by dashing to the capital city with its load of passengers and cargo. Some drivers tooted their horns while passengers waved. I had no doubt in my mind that over the clinging and clanging noises of the vehicle's engine, they would be discussing and drawing conclusions about the identities, motives and state of mind of these two youngsters.

Being that the country was at this time untouched and unspoiled by human greed and concrete disguised as development, the land remained a large swath of green trees and shrubs of which mangoes and wild berries dominated. We carelessly and innocently fed on them to complement the sandwiches and sodas we had. Sometime around 4 p.m. we slid our tired bodies into our home destination at Kpehe, Accra as quietly and unannounced as we had started ten hours ago. Tired, but very satisfied and accomplished.

7

Two Near-Fatal Encounters in College

Cape Coast literally made me into what and who I would be in adulthood.

Cape Coast was as fun a town as Kpandu was. It was here that I would cultivate a fine sense of humor that would serve me well throughout my adult live. Araba, a girl far ahead of her age, opened me up to the pleasures of youthful love, including the sweetness of the forbidden fruit that lay within a woman's curves. I became a fully detribalized Ghanaian in Cape Coast, it being a truly cosmopolitan city that welcomed and accepted all manner of humans without regard to tribe or political orientation.

Like sister Emy and brother Theo before me, I was confirmed into the Christian faith at the Presbyterian Church located on *Jerusalem Hill*, not too far from *London Bridge* that linked *Old Hospital Hill* to places like *Swanzie* and *Chapel Square*. That's Cape Coast for you – the fun city where a culvert is called *London Bridge*, a parched, thirsty open field is named *Victoria Park* and *Queen Ann's Point* is a graveyard!

Cape Coast was and still is Ghana's "education town". A university college and several elitist high schools are located there, more so than in any other town in the country. It was also a popular tourist destination because of an inglorious slave castle/dungeon built by European colonialist to facilitate their execution of the heinous Trans-Atlantic Slave Trade that saw the capture and forced dislocation of millions of Africans from their homeland.

Ghana at this time was carved into nine administrative regions with Cape Coast the capital city of the Central Region. Its streets were therefore littered with students, office workers, tourists and all types of thrill seekers from all over the world. This notwithstanding, it was an easy-going cosmopolitan center -- very friendly and welcoming, little or no crime. Club da Costa (CDC) was the best-known club in town --- a watering hole where all comers gathered to socialize and drink or dance the evenings and their blues away.

One evening as I sat at the counter sipping away on a beer, a young man approached . He looked every bit an American tourist. He had with him three local male youngsters, each trying desperately to outdo the other with their rendition of what they believed to be "American guy ways". He came over to where I was sitting asked to know who I was after he'd introduced himself. As soon as I said my name and that I was a university student, he took my head in both palms and began kissing me full blood in the mouth! For a brief moment I froze. Completely stupefied! When I gathered myself, I pushed the pervert away, swung at him and grabbed a stack of tissue and began spitting and spewing saliva into them. I would have sanded my tongue if I could. All the while, the local nincompoops with him kept clapping and applauding. "Yankee, yankee", they kept babbling like the little brainless piglets in the epic book, "The Animal Farm" who never stopped bleating what they have been taught -- "two legs good, four legs bad!!" They stopped only when they heard me screaming insults at their star performer in words that have no equivalent in the English language. I was mad as hell. I felt dirtied and insulted. To a young man raised in strong Presbyterian traditions of the Akwapim flavor, kissing, like sex itself, is a private and consensual sinful act that everyone commits but no one sees (if pregnancy is not the wages). Not only have my values been violated. It was done by a strange thrill-seeking stranger in the full view of the whole world!! You could surmise that he must be having his way with the local boys -- sexually.

I learned to consume alcohol and developed a strong toleration for it in Cape Coast. Fortunately, it did not come with the cravings that would have made me into an alcoholic.

Accra is where, at age thirteen, I learned to smoke cigarette with the other members of the 39 Steps street gang. One club member stole the cigarettes from his mother's grocery store. I would quit after twenty-two years. I tried marijuana or "wee". It didn't catch my fancy and found it not worth the risk. But Cape Coast is where I perfected cigarette smoking and alcohol consumption.

It was at Winneba that I picked up the nickname "Koliko" by which I would be known for the rest of my life. It started with three of us classmates from the same secondary school being given admission to one school for Sixth Form education -- myself, Vespa and Tommie. Vespa was the first to use the word back in our old school as a code word for cigarette. Anyone with the rudimentary knowledge of the social mores of the time would tell you that smoking was identifying mark of those headed for hell -- never do wells, criminals, thieves, prostitutes, jailbirds etc. If this held true for adults, consider what it meant for teens and youngsters? Society would tolerate an adult pedophile than it would a school kid caught smoking!

To teenagers, to smoke was to be "in". We therefore found ingenious ways to outsmart adults. We knew what "koliko" meant. Adults did not. We could talk openly about cigarette.

When we introduced the term in our new school, I somehow became the word. I do not know why and how. My real name was completely thrown aside. I became Koliko!!

My father once came looking for me by the name he had given me. No one knew G. Anor. I wasn't enrolled in the school, they said. And then he ran into one of my two other buddies. "Oh, it's Koliko" Then everyone around screamed, "Papa, why didn't you say Koliko? Who doesn't know Koliko?" My exasperated father responded: "I did not name him Koliko".

The harder I fought, the deeper the name stuck. I gave up and actually came to love it. I guess it gave me a peculiar and distinct identity.

When I entered the University, Cape Coast University, fondly called Cape Vars, for a three-year undergraduate stint, "Koliko" was firmly entrenched as my nickname.

College life was easy and sweet. A room to myself, weekly supply of toilet paper, three square meals a day with snacks in between and a generous stipend meant for the purchase books. Nobody purchased a magazine with that money. "Millions", as we called it, funded our endemic drinking and sex indulgence and cravings.

A free round the clock transportation service made it extremely easy for students and workers to ride back and forth through campus and town. Being that I was a townsman, I had reason to be in town every day and be a regular passenger on the last bus of the day.

Two incidents during this period stand out in my mind. One incident involved a fellow student who, in error, thought I was hitting on his girlfriend. This was a girl I knew from my elementary school days. After a night out drinking with her and a girlfriend of mine, the girls came to my campus room. She planned to spend the night with her boyfriend, also a student. I agreed to walk the girl to her man's room. We knocked a few times and turned to walk away since he wasn't responding. Then out of nowhere, this burly man busted out of the room like a raging bull. Before I could blink an eye, this creature swung at me. His fist landed squarely on my chin, sending me tumbling from the third floor to the ground floor. The force of the blow, its suddenness and the decent amount of alcohol in me conspired to make me the perfect victim. I fell over the verandah wall like a rag doll thrown from a window that high up. I landed on my back side on a grassy knoll on the side of the concrete floor three floors below. I am unable to explain why my head did not crash unto the concrete floor. I laid there dazed for a minute or two, got up, dusted myself and walked gingerly to my room. The next morning this Nigerian exchange student came to Room 50, my pad, to apologize after he learned of his grievous mistake that could have killed me. I cursed at him and screamed for him to roast his miserable soul in hell. My anger was fueled by two factors: 1. I had been sucker punched and given no chance to retaliate, and 2. I ended up having the two girls spend the night in my room. I didn't get to spend the night with my lady to receive the sexual gratification I had planned for.

It wasn't until several weeks after that I really took in the narrow escape that had come my way. It came to me when I accidentally walked by the spot of the incident. Youthful arrogance and impetuousness allowed me to write it off as "one of those things" and let it slide into sub consciousness. Today, age and life's experiences demand that I ponder a little and ask: "was it accidental, sheer luck or something in between?"

One more near fatal incident would come my way at the university. It took place in a lecture hall at the Department of Education building. It was a one of those hot, hazy, lazy afternoons when you would rather snooze in bed than struggle to make sense of Professor's History of Education lectures. This lecturer was more into reciting his academic credentials than he was about stimulating young minds to find solutions to a myriad of problems facing a young and struggling country. Needless to say, his lectures were always dull and unexciting. The only reason anybody enrolled in this class was because it was a required course. Mandatory, that is.

An old ceiling fan creaked as it turned in a lazily and painfully to circulate stale air in a futile attempt to cool the room. This was huge fan with a bulky base about the size and diameter of drum of a car's wheel. It would be apt to describe it as an old model that Don Diego D'Azambuja must have brought with him when he made contact with Kwamena Ansah on the sandy beaches of Edina in 1472! Anyone on whose head it fell on was as good as dead. We routinely sat directly beneath it without any thought of it ever falling and crushing heads.

Then one day it happened. I sat directly underneath it. Halfway into the lecture, I left the hall supposedly to use the bathroom. Truthfully, I was taking a smoking break. When I came back, the room fell dead silent. Everyone starred in my direction, but nothing was said, and the lecturer went on and on with what I thought was boring stuff. I went back to my seat. Then I saw and understood why I was being stared at. I had barely left the room when the fan broke from its moorings and came crashing below. It broke the chair. The fan blades were all mangled and squished up. The heavy metal drum base cracked. Oil dripped through the crack. It broke and fell directly unto the spot I sat minutes before!!

My mates applauded my luck. Only goodness could tell what would have happened had I been sitting there when the fan fell. I never ever gave it any other thought. College life continued and my happy-go-lucky attitudes continued.

A couple of days later, one of the older members in the class, engaged me.

"What do you think about what happened?"

"What happened?", feigning convenient amnesia.

"You mean the fan incident?"

"Yes", he said. "Won't you go to church and thank God? You are an incredibly lucky chap, you know".

"Go to church?" I exclaimed in astonishment.

" What happened is a big miracle. The mangled blades, that's you head right there".

"Okay, I get it".

"You would have been dead by now had you been sitting there. You leaving the time you did and the fan to collapse that instant is the miracle I'm talking about" .

"You know I went to smoke", that was me, "and you know smoking is bad".

He knew right away where I was heading. "Koliko, Koliko, Koliko, when will you be serious? Nothing means anything to you. You don't take anything serious". He walked away with disbelieve and disgust written all over him.

I added to his disappointment with the words: "the lesson of this incident is that cigarette smoking is a blessing and I should never give it up. It saved my life!".

Pedantic logic!! Such was the carefree attitude and reckless abandonment that attended my days at the university. To me, it was unfiltered fun.

8

Escaping Fatherhood

I left Cape Coast after graduating on schedule with a bachelor's degree in Education. But Cape Coast never left me, even unto this day. I still carry fond memories of a fine city and fine times.

The next port of call for me was Assin Foso, an especially important stop on the circuitous train tracks linking Accra with Kumasi and Takoradi. That was before human-imposed decadence visited Ghana and destroyed even the little infrastructure self-serving British colonialists had built. I was sent there in 1974 to serve out a one-year national service commitment to the nation for the fee free education I had received. I would stay on for four years to teach in this teacher training institution. New challenges, opportunities and experiences, including dodging fatherhood awaited me.

While there weren't major life altering or near-death experiences to recall, Foso is memorable for the assortment of characters I met. Foso was where I met and befriended such guys as Yaw, Willis, and Charles. I cultivated relationships with several females including students I taught, public servants and a slate of local women, one of them called Ama.

If Ama is still alive, she lives with the secret knowledge of who the father of her first girl child is. If she is gone to the world of the ancestors, the secret is interred with her bones.

We had a good relationship going for about a year. I remember Ama to be a very decent woman. Very caring and respectful. She frequented my apartment so often that she seemed to be living there. Suddenly and without warning she stopped coming. She simply dropped off the radar and appeared to have faded into oblivion. No visits, no messages, no communication whatsoever.

I did all I could to find her. She was never there whenever I went looking for her where I knew she lived. None of the friends I knew gave any information as to where and what must have happened to her. Then one day we ran into each other at the market.

"Ama, what did I do to you? Seems you are hiding from me".

She held my hand, led me into her room and closed the door. She pulled off the blouse she was wearing to show a shining stomach full of a baby. She was pregnant!

My mouth fell open.

"You see this", she said. "I am five months pregnant with your baby".

"What?!!!", I exclaimed.

"Owura, don't panic", she said with a calm demeanor. Of course she saw the panic written all over me.

"Just listen to me".

I braced for the worst.

"Yes, I am carrying your baby. But I also know a few things. You are a young, up and coming man from the big city. This is not where you want to end up. You have big plans for yourself and your future. I am a village lady with elementary education. You will not want me for a wife, today or tomorrow".

She paused for effect. "Am I lying?"

"Continue", I said feebly with my head bowed.

"I know well enough not to saddle you with any commitments in this village. I have found me a local man. He is well to do and can take care of us. I've given him the pregnancy and he has accepted it. But the baby is yours".

What was I to do? Get mad or be happy? The lady was dead right on the money. At 26, I was not about to settle yet, let alone with a someone we, educated brats, derisively saw as a village "wench".

"But why d-d-d-didn't you t-t-tell me?" suddenly stuttering in speech.

"I told you why. Don't be upset. Only you and I know. Our secret. Go on. Live your life and let me live mine in this village".

If I could, I would have faked some tears. But I couldn't. A part of me, the bigger bratty part smiled inside and said: "Thank you" and walked out of her room in the four squared family houses in this noisy midway town.

About two years would pass before I would ran into Ama at the local market. She pulled me aside to a less noisy corner and said:

" Your girl has taken her first steps. Won't you buy her eggs?"

Offering eggs in Akan culture is recognition and celebration of significant achievements or milestones in one's life. For a child, first steps, circumcision (for boys), first menstruation are classic milestones.

I gave Ama more than was enough to buy a crate of eggs! Our paths never crossed again -- mother and child, "my child?".

One of the supervisors under whom I worked was a character to remember for all the wrong reasons. The academic credentials of this forty-four-year-old fellow were a bachelor's degree and a certificate in teaching English to foreign learners earned from participation a one-year training program in Britain. His greatest delight was to recite ad infinitum his experiences in Britain during the one year stay for the TOEFL training. Give him a noun and a verb and he will fill in the blank with nothing more than "when I was in London , when I was in London!" To think he was there for barely a year!!

The twice divorced Ol'Grey and I kicked off on the wrong side of each other. I showed up for work one day later than I was supposed to. Lack of a means of transportation was the one and only reason. This was the time that Ghana had begun its downward economic spiral following the ill-fated coup by Colonel Acheampong. The economic downturn would thrust Ghana into all kinds of bad social, political and moral labyrinths had begun. To this day, the country is still struggling to maneuver its way out of the mess.

Whereas I expected Ol'Grey to give me some form of warning or even cut me a break (being a first offender and considering my age, inexperience, first job blues, transportation issues), what he gave me went far and beyond any sensible reprimand. He put a bad write-up in my file and gave me a tongue lashing that I wouldn't tolerate from anyone, including my father.

"You will never say these nonsenses to me ever again", I said and stormed out of his office.

And with that we hardly said anything to one another for the entire four years that I worked in that institution. Ol'Grey could not stand me. I had no love for him either. And he nearly had the last laugh in our game of mutual dislike for each other when years later he attempted to destroy a dream career a bank offered me.

It was at Foso that I found the Baha'i Faith, a religion that I credit with filling me in on some of the questions that my Christian upbringing had left unanswered. No, ignored.

It was introduced to me by a colleague for whom I still reserve the utmost respect. I found in Baha'i very logically reasonable answers to questions that plagued my restless youthful mind -- who created the God that created the world; does God really possess all the qualities that have been assigned him (omnipresence, omniscience, omnipotence etc.)? If he does, why would he look on as people commit the most heinous of crimes, injustices etc. in the world and most times get away with them? Is Jesus God? What about the other Great Religions and their founders? Is Jesus coming a second time? If he is, when, where and how? Resurrection, Judgment or Re-incarnation? On and on and on the queries tumbled and rumbled in my head. The Christian faith into which I had been born and raised imposed a terse injunction for inquiring minds such as mine: do not question or attempt to understand, just believe. In other words, come into this faith with your brains neatly tucked away in an iron cage for it wouldn't help you. It would rather impede your spiritual progress. This is not to say that Christianity did not have the answers, or at least some of them. Just That we were taught not to ask or seek!

When I found Baha'i, I found answers to some of the questions (certainly not all) that informed my skepticism about the Christian brand I had been taught. I came to honor and respect all religions, all mankind better. Ironically, Christianity became more meaningful and relevant to me than it had ever been. I travelled all over Ghana with Iranians (where Baha'i originated), British/Irish/Scottish men and women, Americans, other Africans preaching and teaching in a genuine effort to proselytize Ghana.

It was at this period that I met and became friends with individuals like Pauline, a Catholic school teacher. It is the finest platonic relationship I would ever be in. She had a son, Paul, fathered by the American priest (father?) of the Parish that ran the school she worked at. She would tell in graphic detail how the supposed celibate priest would slip into her room late at night in disguise to conduct his unholy business. Pauline was so sweet and kind that it was not too difficult to understand why she had been preyed on by a man who took his "fatherly" duties rather too literally.

I credit Baha'i with confirming in me a belief in the pursuit of knowledge as a required exercise in one's spiritual development, rather than as an impediment.

Accra changed all that when I moved there in 1978. The first casualty was the relationship I had going with my high school sweetheart. I remain regretful of the manner in which I left her. I admit to having committed an egregious offence for which Hannah may probably never forget or forgive me.

We became sweethearts when we met in high school. She was five years my junior. As a consequence of her dad being a Christian minister, the tall smashing beauty was very well raised in Christian faith and traditions. Seven fantasy years later, I swore openly and in secret that I had found my life's partner. At age twenty-six, I held myself matured and ready enough to propose to marry her. I probably was all that and more. Baha'i Faith had come into my life, setting off what I saw as a spiritual transformation and its attendant down-toning of a hitherto wild youth.

I bought a gold-plated ring, a Bible, two bottles of schnapps, a bottle of wine, went down to her father in another part of the country and promised to take his daughter's hand in marriage within one year.

It would not be. The glitz and glamour of Accra seduced me. It won over the little spiritual character Baha'i Faith had helped me acquire. With her in Kumasi, she could conveniently be taken to be out of sight and therefore out of mind. I could live with my benign neglect of her and a woeful disregard for the moral responsibilities I had consciously and willfully assumed when I promised to marry her. I fell and with it, whatever goodies and or glitches that would have come with a journey on life's highway with Hannah.

If she'd forgiven me and moved on with a worthier man, why, I would smile and be eternally grateful. If not, I know, she, in rightful indignation, would have me condemned to suffer in the hottest part of hell. I will forever pray for the former but would not deny her the latter.

All I knew about the nation's central bank before securing a job there were the things in textbooks, I read on the way to passing the required courses in Economics so as to acquire a college degree. I had never seen the imposing architectural structure located on Accra's High Street that housed the institution that handled the country's monetary affairs.

My first ever trip to the place was at the behest of a friend wanting to check on the status of his employment application.

"Why don't you drop one in there yourself?", Arday (the friend) advised rhetorically.

I did and was offered employment after three grueling interviews. Arday never made it past the first.

My destiny, luck, sheer coincidence, accident or what?

9

The Bright Lights of Accra

The nation's central bank -- the equivalent of America's Federal Reserve Bank -- offered me a junior management position after three grueling interviews in September 1978. I had successfully taken the mandatory medical examination and was two days removed from reporting for work.

Then I received a letter from the bank. It said the bank had decided to withdraw the employment offer. They were sorry, the letter said but I should not report for duty as arranged. I am unable to describe the devastation that consumed me. Who or what could have caused this? Could it be a mistake? Did they detect something medically wrong with me? How could one be fired before he is employed? Could this be a trick someone was playing or a case of mistaken identity?

After hours and days of thoughts that led nowhere, I came to the conclusion that it was an error. The letter was meant for someone else on staff who had a similar name. And somehow, our names and addresses got mixed up and the wrong person was served. Otherwise who ever heard of a person fired before he is employed?

"Mr. Anor, the Bank is extremely sorry for everything that's happened. We made an awfully bad mistake", the personnel manager told me when I went to enquire.

Okay. That sounds good. They are admitting to have a committed a grievous error after all. Everything will be straightened up. Happy thoughts floated in my head.

Things were straightened up all right but not how I expected.

"The employment letter should not have been sent at all. The Board declined your application", he said." We are deeply sorry".

Huh? I gasped silently. "But sir, I made it to the third and final interview which am told was merely a formality".

"What did I do wrong".

"The Board reserves the right to employ and fire whomever it chooses", the manager said rather coldly.

"So sir what am I to do", doing my best to hold back tears. "I quit my job and have moved my family from Foso to Accra and now I am out of work?"

Not exactly accurate. I had no family then and I hadn't quit my job yet!

"If you wish, you can write a petition to the Board. Maybe they will reconsider. That's all you can do. Good luck".

Petition? Okay. I would do as the man suggested, though I had no believe it would work. These are people who would fire before employing you!!

The petition I sent said the things I could say:

a. I had quit my job.

b. I had become unemployed and therefore had no means of supporting myself and my family.

c. I had moved my myself and my family to Accra at costs I wouldn't have incurred if not for the offer.

A response took what seemed like eternity to come. It was a very torturing time, as torturing as awaiting the results a of blood test after sleeping with a woman who died of AIDS!

Meanwhile I had crawled back to my old job, distraught and sobered. I encountered a somewhat friendlier Ol'Grey. He smiled at me more often and assigned me responsibilities he never would have. He actually offered me a ride in his rickety old car to Cape Coast to follow up on my application for graduate studies at the University

What could account for this change in attitude? I wondered. With nothing to hang it on, I took it as one of those things. Maybe with so few young graduate teachers like me to go round, he had woken to the value that I brought into the instructional staff pool.

Boy, was I wrong! Apparently, that old creep knew he had done the devil's due and was certain I wasn't going anywhere. Asked for a testimonial on me in his capacity as my supervisor, he had submitted a damning, scathing commentary on my person and character, one that would make even my mother deny me for a son! So he was in fact delivering a "gotcha, sucker" message anytime he smiled or winked my way.

I would know what he had done when I eventually went to work for the Bank. About a month after the withdrawal letter, the Bank wrote to withdraw the withdrawal letter and re-offer me employment once again.

My petition had worked!!

I would learn later that my appeal was all but lost until one board member came to my aid and argued over a testimonial that he thought was anything but objective. They would give a benefit of the doubt opportunity to prove or disprove Ol'Grey's damning testimonials.

Instead of the regular six months probationary period, I would serve one year. Instead of three years satisfactory service, I would earn promotion after four years of more than satisfactory rating. These conditions were posted in my file and all my supervisors knew about them. I took the offer and went on to work very satisfactorily in this prestigious institution for four years. I left Foso with the widest smile on my face and the middle finger in Ol'Grey's!

But Ol'Grey wasn't done with me. About three months after starting at the bank, I get called into the office of the chief legal officer who went by the title of Secretary. He pulled a letter out of a drawer and read the contents. It said among other things that I had abandoned my job at the school and was in violation of a legal bond to the Ministry of Education. The bank should therefore terminate my appointment and have me returned to post immediately!

Anger or fear? I do not know what the Secretary read in my face when he, speaking like the lawyer he was, said:

"Go, take care of your problems and show me evidence when done", he said and waved me out of his office.

I returned to mine and pulled out a copy of the letter I had sent to the Ministry serving the required notice of resigning the teaching job. I hadn't deserted as Ol'Grey alleged.

I signed a contract to serve the Ghana government in any capacity it would assign for two years. This was required of all college graduates who had enjoyed free education at public expense. I had served four years, well over my contractual obligations.

So, where was Ol'Grey's beef? I showed a copy of the resignation letter to the Secretary and never heard anything about this matter ever again.

Here I was again -- a beneficiary of protection from the snarls of the fowler that prowls by day and the pestilence that flies by night!

I spent four years at the bank, years of mixed fortunes, career successes and serious character failures whose outcomes are still with me. Within a couple of years from when I started, I had been voted the secretary of the senior staff association. In that capacity, I and my executives would organize the first ever life concert in the bank and lead a protest strike against policies that we considered unfair and discriminatory against management staff. I owned a car, serviced the most powerful in-house committee, gone overseas on a bank sponsored working trip and had become a favorite of the then head of the institution. I met and struck some very memorable friendships with both men and women. A few also loathed and disliked me. Of course! It would be stupid to think I had just friends and no enemies. I dated some of the hottest and controversial ladies there was. However, had I known what hand fate was dealing me in the form of one of the women I met and fell in love with, I would have run to the farthest end of the world and confined myself to a hermit's existence. I did not and my life's trajectory was altered forever. It was at this time that I abandoned Baha'i. I went from a world of relative innocence and naivety into a soap opera one ruled by hard core arrogance, self-centeredness, shamelessness and greed.

10

United States, Here I Come!

Before I knew, I was on a bus bound for Nigeria, a heart broken victim of deception and betrayal. That would be my first trip to the African giant of a nation. I tracked down my old school mate Kofi B who had moved there and was teaching in a number of colleges in Lagos. The sprawling city was a boiling cauldron of millions of humanity thrown in by the basest of instincts -- survival. I stayed for a week. The shock of what I experienced jolted my senses and woke me up from my emotional slumber. I retraced my steps back to Accra to the soap opera world of kill and or be killed, literally.

A year after, in 1981, the decision was made to travel to Nigeria a second time, this time in pursuit of a visa that would enable me to enter the United States of America. The girl that I believed then that I loved had relocated there and I was hell bent on joining her. With the visa application denied in Accra, where else to go than Nigeria, which with its oil fortunes had become the darling of the western nations!

Four years passed before I would secure the precious permit. In that process, I met a fine Ghanaian nurse who became the mother of my first child, a girl I named after my mother.

When I left Ghana to go to Nigeria, I became one in the throng of thousands of Ghanaians seeking relief from the travails of a failing state brought on by half-baked "revolutions" led by Akyeampong and Rawlings that inarguably destroyed Ghana politically, economically and maybe spiritually too. Everyone who could, young and old, firm and infirm, man, woman and child, religious and atheist left the country in droves to go anywhere – anywhere on God's planet but Ghana.

Dr Kwame Nkrumah had taken on the mantle of leadership during and following the struggle for independence and self-rule by some eight million people that live in a country constructed by British imperialists. They, i.e. the British usurpers, called it the Gold Coast colony, one of several possessions that Europeans would create then abrogate and arrogate unto themselves under some devise called colonialism that when stripped of any niceties amount to nothing more than bullying and stealing. Bullying and stealing it was because the perpetrators did what they did for no other reasons other than 1. they could; 2. were militarily stronger and 3. took what belonged to others without permission. When the victims protested, they were brutally suppressed, sometimes to the point of genocidal extermination as happened Hottentots of South Africa, the Australian Aborigines and Native Peoples of the Americas. This is colonialism in plain and simple language.

Nkrumah changed Gold Coast into Ghana and attempted to build a modern nation that would, among other things, be a model of the African's ability to handle his own affairs. Over the years, Ghana would ironically become an example of the African's ability to mishandle his own affairs! Soldier boys Kotoka, Afrifa and other armchair warriors led the way. They sold their oath of loyalty to foreign interests for a stack of dollars and chased Nkrumah out of office after just about four years. A junta made up police and military officers calling itself the National Liberation Council gutted all of Nkrumah's progressive developmental programs and set the tone for years of economic decay that were to come. Busia and Akuffo Addo who spoke Greek better than Greeks, became the Prime Minister and President of a reticent Second Republic doomed to fail at birth. An opportunistic rough soldier Kutu Akyeampong staged his coup and took over for no other reason than to restore the "few benefits" soldiers enjoyed that Busia had abolished. That was his major complaints! He more than restored those benefits (which included access to women's reproductive organs). He epitomized what incompetence, indiscipline, cluelessness in high places could do to a nation.

Mess hall soldiers consumed by a false sense of self-worth and piety. One soldier after another made attempts at forcibly taking over political power. Kotoka kicked out Nkrumah. Arthur took out Kotoka. Akyeampong did in Busia. Akuffo removed Akyeampong. Rawlings killed Akuffo and others, so on and so forth. Get the picture? These events and episodes set the stage for junior army officer John Rawlings, the son of a Scottish man and a Ghanaian woman to take the nation on a long rough ride to further ruin. But for brief two-year interregnum of emptiness served by a President Hilla Liman in the Third Republic democratic experiment, Ghana suffered twenty plus years of a philosophically bankrupt "Rawlings revolution". By the 1980s, Ghana was firmly entrapped in a social, political, but mostly economic quagmire worsened by brutal military dictatorship. Anyone with head on his head and the minutest of an ant's skill to sell sought to leave the country in pursuit of opportunities to sell that skill for a better life anywhere in the world. As providence would have it, here was Nigeria, less than a day's trip away enjoying colossal economic prosperity from its oil fortunes.

All manner of human characters from all over the universe --- firm or infirm, sane or insane, broken or mended, savage or civilized, tamed or wild, priest or prostitute --- made a wild dash to Nigeria, the El-Dorado (gold mine) of our time

Nigeria came to be summed up in one word in Ghanaian thought: "Agege". Agege, a massive sprawling slum suburb in Lagos (then the capital city of this giant Nigeria) was virtually the first port of call for nearly all would-be migrants. Lagos itself was a very apt summation of the wide range of contrasts and contradictions Nigeria presented -- extreme wealth and abject poverty, beauty and beastly ugliness, tolerance and extreme xenophobia, polarization and plurality, euphoria and danger.

When I left to go to Nigeria, I did not exactly fit the profile of a typical Ghanaian economic refugee. The overwhelming majority of young Ghanaians had gone to Nigeria for economic reasons --- un/under employment, depressed incomes, poor social infrastructures, etc. I had no such reason(s). I was a rising star, securely employed in a prestigious banking institution in the country. I had a very decent balance in my Barclays Bank account. I had invested some hundreds more in my brother's import forwarding/clearing business. The Peugeot 404 salon car I owned, though not swanky, was the envy of many a young man of my age and class. I lived in exceptionally fine circumstances in what was then a prime Accra neighborhood. My future, as far as career advancement goes, looked very secured and promising. I held a junior management position in the country's central bank establishment.

The pursuit of a United States visa was what took me to Nigeria. Period! The US Embassy in Ghana had rejected my visa application.

Just as I pondered how to proceed, here comes Kenneth, a Lagos based friend. Kenneth had moved to Nigeria two years earlier. A graduate of Accra Polytechnic in building construction, he was working for a foreign architectural firm, one of several chipping what they could off Nigeria's oil wealth to the detriment of the welfare of the people. He happened to be returning to Lagos after a short vacation and was all too willing to have me tag along.

Apese, a sprawling fishing village near Lagos was my first port of call. One night there and I knew that this visa quest in this country wasn't going to be as breezy as I had thought. Of all the strange and bizarre sights and sounds none left a lasting mark in my memory than what I encountered the very first morning. I asked to be shown the toilet to do the obvious.

"Toilet?", he asked. The expression on his face betrayed what he was thinking --- you spoiled, uppity African black man behaving like *oyibo (white man)*.

"There are no toilets here. But I will show you where you can do your business".

We walked around a number of aluminum sheet structures and came to a white sandy beach that stretched as far as the eyes could see. There, on the sandy turf in the misty dawn weather were about a hundred or so men, women and children squatting and relieving their bellies and intestines of digestion's wastes!

Kenneth looked my way and nodded as if to say, "this is it – make your choice; your belly or your pride". I found a spot and squatted. Right in that instant, a young woman, one that I would've loved to date walked up a few feet in front, drew down what she was wearing and began her business of emptying her anal and vaginal cavities! I was dumbfounded, shocked, stupefied, confused.

"What happened to female decency? Self-pride? Devalued womanhood? It introduced me to how cheap Ghanaian womanhood had become in Nigeria. You could have them for as cheap as one naira!! That was how much it cost to have "one round" sex with the hundreds of sex workers in Nigerian cities.

It nevertheless wasn't enough to jolt me back to Ghana. The US visa pull was stronger and a mere indecent exposure could not drag me away. I resolved to look for somewhere other than Lagos/Apese to move to. I hopped on a bus bound for Oyan, a town on the border of Oyo and Kwara states. I intended to hook up with a friend who left three years earlier and was teaching at a state educational institution. Yaw was his name. With his help, I found work as the head of English Department of a grammar school. The pay was better than good, especially if measured along the exceedingly low cost of living in Nigeria at the time. Unless one entered into some type of "tails you lose, heads I win" raffle with the devil, there was no way you could expend a month's salary on rent, food, clothing, transportation and entertainment. Nigeria was indeed a working man's paradise. The pay was more than good while the work that went with it presented the easiest of challenges.

Life was good. Teaching the rules of the Queen's language to high school kids, holding faculty meetings, playing soccer and staying up late drinking beer with my buddies was as heavenly as a mouse taking residence under a New York City subway train track! As and when the suppliers of electricity -- N.E.P.A (acronym for *Nigeria Electricity & Power Authority* but derisively twisted into *Never Expect Power Always* for obvious reasons) -- would permit and televisions become operable, we would watch alongside the beer, reruns of very old European and American shows that colonized our minds and imagination and whetted our desires to die for a chance to live in the white man's world.

Then one day in the second year, my paycheck would not be cashed by the local bank. The bank officials asked to see me in person. The standard practice had been that our salaries were paid directly into our individual accounts for us to take out as and when we desired. We never had any problems with our personal checks being cashed for us by messengers while we worked. Asking to see me in person was therefore quite strange. I went nonetheless, thinking nothing of anything beyond maybe a faulty signature. I was ushered into an office and offered a seat. About five different persons came in at different times and asked for some form of identification. After waiting for about thirty minutes, someone came in with my money and said I could leave. No reason, excuse or apology given. I kept my anger and disgust to myself and left without uttering a word.

The next day, one of the townsfolk who had taken a liking for Ghanaians (he was born, raised and employed in Ghana prior to an ill-conceived and executed compliance order that threw millions of resident immigrants out of Ghana) came to me with the advice that I should not under any circumstance spend the coming weekend in town, specifically in my house.

"Oga English", he said in his pidgin English drawl, *"make you na comot from town this Saturday ooo. Make you no sleep for house ooo. Ibi say na wahala de come for you oo".* He was advising me, *Oga English,* (a *Master English* title given because I taught English) to skip town because trouble was coming my way.

What *"wahala"* (mayhem) and why? I asked and got no answer. I had lived in this country long enough to take him seriously. Smart kids, it is said, are spoken to in parables. I came back on Monday morning to find my room broken into and comprehensively trashed. Nothing was missing, making it evident that this was no burglary. Days later, word got around about how **Oga English** had literally dodged the bullet. Had the night hunters caught up with him, he would be singing halleluiah chorus to his maker. Dead, that is!

All town knew whose handiwork it was, but no one could prove or even dare say it. The night hunters were feared vigilante night prowlers who did anything from community policing to revenge justice which could be anything from beatings, warnings, extortion to outright killings. Apparently, someone had a contracted them to take care of me. Why?

Word got around once again. It was for the very same reason or reasons that some allege got Adam thrown out of the Garden of Eden, started the Trojan war, got David to plot Uriah's death and Samson to have his hair clipped and eventually killed. I dated a girl who, unbeknown to me, was dating the son of a powerful chief, a young man who worked at the bank where I kept the money which was the money I was paid for the job I did for the government

Herein lies an explanation of the summons I got from the bank weeks before. It indeed was merely a ruse to have me positively identified to ensure that the right man was had. I owed my escape and survival to Ajayi, the guy who pre-warned me to skip town.

Ajayi's parents had settled in Ghana for many years. In fact, he was born in a little farming town in the forest area of Ghana. He had received free elementary education through the forward-looking policies of the legendary Ghanaian leader Osagyefo Dr Kwame Nkrumah. Before the ill-advised Aliens Compliance law enacted by Kofi Busia in 1969, Ajayi thought of himself as a Ghanaian. That harsh eviction of his kith and kin notwithstanding, he loved Ghana and Ghanaians. He was married to his Ghanaian girlfriend from high school and took frequent trips there to visit "his family". He would have no one harm any of us if he could help it. He had gotten wind of the deadly "lesson" planned for me. He couldn't stop it, but he could snitch, and it is by him that I live to tell my story.

I lived on in the area for two additional years, picking up vital experiences in places such as Oshogbo, Igbaye, Ijabe, Inisa, Ikirun, Offa, Ede, Ogbomosho, Oyan, Oro, Ilesha, Okuku and far more famous places as Illorin, Ile Ife, Ibadan, Abeokuta and Lagos and Kano where I eventually secured the almighty US visa.

All told, I spent four happy-not-so-happy-years in Nigeria and would have stayed for more had it not been for a decision by the powers that be to dispense of the services of all non-Nigerian expatriates in its employ. All undocumented *aliens (illegal non-Nigerians)* were ordered by the ruling military dictatorship to leave town. We had overstayed our welcome. All *aliens*, especially Ghanaians, had to go! Payback time, a reverse of a similar bad act by the Ghanaian government in 1969. The then administration headed by Kofi Busia passed a reprehensible Aliens Compliance Act which essentially sought to throw millions of Nigerian migrant residents out of Ghana.

For many of us caught in this foolish tit-for-tat game, going back to Ghana was not a viable option. For one thing, it amounted to an admission of failure. Our friends who stayed behind would laugh in our faces for having gambled and lost.

More importantly, with Flight Lieutenant Jerry John Rawlings at the height of his revolutionary drum march that had the country's economy caught in a terrible chicken dance, Ghana was the least of places one wanted to go back to.

Having lost my teaching job, I revived my original reason for going to Nigeria, i.e. to secure a United States visa. The fuel that fired that desire had receded over the years. Easy living was to blame. I had gotten into a relationship with a fine Ghanaian nurse in Ilorin. Our first daughter was born on May 13, 1985 and life was good.

I could apply for the visa at the American Embassy in Lagos or the Consulate in Kaduna. I chose to go to Kaduna, three hundred miles and a whole day's road journey from Ilorin where I lived at this time.

The entire process of submitting the application, being interviewed and told to go pay the visa fee must have taken all of forty minutes to complete. Walking out of the building into the hot, humid and hazy mid-morning Kaduna weather, was probably the happiest moment in my life, albeit a minute or two! I was consumed by an overwhelming sense of accomplishment.

"Yeah, yeah, yeah! I've done it !!

If this is how this how it felt to be in heaven, I had died and gotten there many times over.

I was literally floating on air. I wished I could pin a banner on my chest proclaiming: "America Bound!! Soon" All Kaduna must step to the side for me to pass through. Couldn't they tell I was about to go America? Should I paste the visa on my forehead so I could be given the special treatment I deserve? That's what going to America meant in our world.

The twelve-hour journey back to my Ilorin base afforded me enough time to take stock of what the visa quest had cost me: 1. a secured future working at the central bank in Accra.

2. four years of mixed fortunes in Nigeria.

3. several hundred Naira paid to "connection men" with contacts that would scuttle the process and help secure the visa. One such men was called Issa, a security guard at the German Embassy in Lagos. My friend Kenneth had connected me to this guy who had sure-fire connections at the American Embassy that could secure me the visa. The asking fee was eight hundred naira – five hundred for the visa and three hundred for a Nigerian passport. My Ghanaian passport was a no-no. The passport with my new name *Asori Anor* was delivered as promised. I could keep Anor, which meant cat in an Igbo. *Asori* was coined out of my Ofori middle name. Neither the visa nor the deal money ever came my way. As is the case with most shady deals, there were no guarantees or refunds. Add to this the cost of countless trips to Lagos and four years of my prime adult years.

Was it worth my while?

11

Starting All Over in New York

A huge British Airways metal bird of an airplane touched down at the JFK airport in New York City around eleven on a cool early September morning in 1985. It flew from Gatwick AirPort in the old back country well known for imperialistic adventures around the world. United Kingdom, that is. In its belly sat yours sincerely, then thirty-five years old. The visa authorization stamped in my passport said I was visiting the United States for vacation travel and would return to my place of origin after whatever months I would be given upon arrival. It had taken me four years to secure this precious visa, the pursuit of which brought me from my native village in Ghana to Lagos to Ibadan to Oshogbo to Okuku then to Kaduna, all in the mighty federated nation of Nigeria.

To mask my real travel intentions I spent two weeks in London with Cousin Eric who had moved there in earlier years, a political refugee and victim of a vicious revolution raging in Ghana at the time. Rawling's revolution, that is. The purpose of the stopover was to buy new clothes, pick up whatever one could to exude an air of a seasoned well-travelled fella with no intentions of overstaying his visa. This was in addition to making sure that one travelled exceptionally light and carried nothing that would give away any intention to overstay. Things like certificates, testimonials, references and the like were red flags that could give you away. I did not carry any. The miniature portmanteau contained a few clothing and small wooden carvings meant as gifts for my hosts. Those items played into the stereotypical notions that when you travel from Africa, you must bring along carvings to gift away. So I carried a few.

My lady host could not take off from work to pick me up from the airport and had made arrangements with a friend to be the welcoming party. Lamore and I hit it off instantly. A graduate of Kwame Nkrumah University of Science and Technology, Lamore had migrated to this place five years earlier and was driving a cab to support whatever it was he intended to do with himself. He was as funny as hell. Lamore zipped his beat down car through the mid-morning New York traffic like a snake slithering through an African swampy undergrowth in search of a rat to snatch for dinner. Boy, was I was mightily impressed! I murmured silently to himself: "wow! is this guy a Ghanaian?" I couldn't wrap my mind around how a Ghanaian could expertly maneuver a car around a scary metal and concrete jungle like New York. It was nothing short of a miracle. When the car pulled up in front of house on tree-lined street in a middle- class neighborhood in Queens, I surely dreamt of the day when I would be like Lamore!

My lady host, one with whom I had a romantic relationship prior to both of us departing Ghana, lived with two other female friends, one of whom had a daughter. They shared what was technically a one-bedroom apartment. But as was typical with exploitative landlords, part of the kitchen had been walled off to create a dubious room large enough to hold a bed and a table. The nursing mother had that room. The rest of us shared the main bedroom.

If you could call it a honeymoon, it lasted for no more than two weeks. But it wasn't for any incendiary flare ups or breakdown in communication. It was due to the harsh realities of economics in the brutally unforgiving western world. I had to find work. I could not stay home and expect others to take care of living expenses such as food, housing, phone usage, and other utilities.

And so began my search for a job, a search that will bring me face to face with how things work great country. I will come to know the subtleties of a what drives virtually the entire lives of a people in virtually every conceivable way, a very intrusive phenomena that operates to keep a certain people beneficiaries of untold privileges and others on the marginal fringes of humanity. I will, for the first time in my life come to know that my melanin-loaded skin color rather than the content of my character was going to be the yardstick by which I was going to be judged in this incredibly advanced country. I came to understand the meaning of Dr, Martin Luther King's plea to be judged not by the color of his skin but by the content of his character.

I would purchase the New York Times newspaper each morning and spend hours perusing and circling job postings that I felt suited my educational qualifications and work experiences -- college degree, managerial/supervisory experiences, teaching , human resource administration etc. There were tons of postings for which I considered myself more than qualified for. But I had forgotten two things, namely, my visa said, "employment unauthorized" and secondly, I am as black as an African can be. It didn't take long to notice a pattern. I would call and get invited for an interview or test. Upon showing up, I would be told very politely that:

a)   the position was filled a short while ago or
b)   you were over/under qualified or
c)   your references could not be reached or
d)   your credentials are foreign or any ridiculous reason good enough for them not to be accused of scuttling the country's equal opportunity employment laws.

Those bastards!

Days turned into weeks and the pattern continued until one day a frustrated host sat me down to a schooling session. "You don't suppose it is by accident that you can't find work at the places you have been looking. Neither should you think it's just because you have not been lucky. There is a reason why almost every Ghanaian you meet is not working at those places you are looking. Many of us are all as educated as you are. Wake up , smell the coffee and come off your high horse. This is racist America", she concluded angrily. That was the first time I was hearing that "smell the coffee" expression. It would not be the last.

Then it struck me. Yes. Nearly all the guys and gals I'd met were taxi drivers, hotel maids or housemen, security guards. shop attendants, fast food workers, home care attendants. Menial jobs, that is. Very few had middle income jobs in medical professions. Many were enrolled in colleges part time, hoping that American education of sorts would be their tickets to upper social mobility in subsequent years.

I recall how one particular individual, William, left such a strong imprint on my memory. William was a very good-looking young man from somewhere in the Ashanti region of Ghana. He had completed sixth form, a two-year pre-college course equivalent to an American associate degree graduation. In fact, his grades were such that he had been offered admission to a bachelor's degree program on a full government scholarship, that paid for everything including a stipend to be expended as one pleased. William declined the offer when a US visa came calling. Images of glorious lifestyles seen in movies and print materials lured him into dreaming of heavenly existences in America. William bit the bait to serve in the supposed American heaven rather than secure college education in his native country. I would ran into several many "Williamses".

Once prompted, I began to search in the right places and soon an opportunity came calling in the form of a temporary paper delivery man. Job description : deliver reams of printing papers to various government offices scattered all over the city of New York. My work tools were a handcart and physical strength, a far cry away from the brain, pen, paper and chalk tools needed to teach in a high school in Nigeria. Each morning, I would load a truck with boxes of printing papers and deliver to designated government offices all over the city. It was a physically demanding job but the pay was relatively good -- a whopping $7 per hour as against the prevailing minimum wage of $3.75 But it lasted for only two weeks, it being a fill-in for the permanent employee on vacation.

This was followed almost immediately by another temporary job, a houseman position at a hotel that was going out of business and required extra hands to pull down structures and remove trash. It was a very physical assignment that also came with good wages determined by a union contract.

Then came a long spell of unemployment. Either by a conspiracy of fate and bad luck or what, nothing came my way for months. I'd dropped off applications at some of the businesses known to employ "illegal alien" labor , namely fast-food places, security providers, hotels, retail shops, etc.

It therefore felt as a god-sent relief when a prestigious Manhattan department store giant invited me for an interview that included a polygraph (lie detector) test for a security guard position. I had submitted an application which among other things, claimed I was a US citizen from St Thomas US Virgin Islands. This, together with a fake Social Security number were ruses intended to circumvent the "employment unauthorized" visa condition.

I showed up promptly at the interview venue with absolutely no idea of what a polygraph test entailed. An aptitude test, perhaps. Or maybe a physical endurance test, being that I was going to be hired to do work that was physically demanding.

Down a short flight of steps I descended to this room in the basement of a huge office building. A burly but friendly man sat me next to a machine that had several wires with rings at the ends. My fingers were slipped into the ring. The administrator explained that the wires picked up and transmitted sensory impulses as the candidate responded to questions asked.

" Please stay as calm as you can. Just say 'yes' or 'no' to my questions. Do not say anything if you do not understand the question. Tell me when you are ready, and we can begin".

"Okay", shifting in the chair.

"Is your name Gaddiel?"

"Yes"

"A US citizen?"

"Yes"

"You from Charlotte Amalie?".

"No".

"Ever been to a place by that name?"

"No".

"Were you born in St Thomas?"

"Yes".

"Do you have a green card?"

"Yes".

"Do you have a social security number?"

"Yes."

"Have you been truthful so far?"

"Yes".

And so ended the test.

The administrator took a look at the sweaty beads formed on my forehead and smilingly quipped: "Don't worry. This is not an immigration department office". He needed not add that I had flunked the test.

I hurried up the stairs as fast as my feet could let me, hoping that the comment about immigration was indeed true. Then it struck me: why hadn't I done a little research on St Thomas before going for the test? I headed straight to a library and took out an encyclopedia. Charlotte Amarlie is indeed the original name of St Thomas! And then coming from there, I would have been in possession of a US passport, never a green card!

Five months flew by and I hadn't done anything and gotten paid, other than those two short temp assignments: the longest stretch ever in my adult life. My host's finances were getting tight and signs of tension were becoming apparent. Something, anything, had to give before the unthinkable happened.

My lady host took me to go see the late Robert Hackman (may his soul rest in peace), a well-known and accomplished Ghanaian in the area at the time. He held the position of store manager of an immensely popular Jewish-owned restaurant in the city. His joint was located at the iconic Grand Central Terminal. It indeed was a big deal for an African immigrant to hold such a position at such a prime location in New York City in the United States of the 1980s. Prior to migrating to the United States, Uncle Bob (that's how he was fondly known) had achieved fame as an athlete, a long-distance runner, had represented Ghana at several international competition and won medals and set records that stayed on the books for a long time. His character and personality earned even more respect within the Ghanaian community in New York. He was kind, friendly and of amiable disposition. He would provide the necessary introductions and references needed for a job hiring thereby making him into a great benefactor to many. He did this freely out of the goodness of his heart.

Traveling on the wings of Uncle Bob's telephone introductions, I strolled confidently into the company's head offices somewhere on Bruckner Boulevard in the Bronx hoping to be hired for a managerial position, considering what I saw as an impressive record of education and work experiences listed on the application form.

An interview with Ralph, the personnel manager followed. "Well, I see here you have college education and have held managerial positions", Ralph said.

"Quite impressive", he went on. "Unfortunately, I don't have any openings for management personnel. I am looking for floor workers."

"Who are floor workers?', I asked.

"They wash and clean floors, ovens and machines and pack products into freezers and delivery trucks", Ralph responded. "Obviously, you are over-qualified for that job but that's what I have. You can take it now and later apply for management trainee position when one opens up".

The pay was an hourly rate of only $3.15, sixty cents lower than the prevailing legal minimum wage. Take-it-or-leave-it! That's it! Taking it came with a very severe hit to my psyche; a crushing fall from respectable job in prestigious Bank in Ghana to a miserable less-than-minimum menial job. Rejecting it meant going back home to face the justified wrath of a girlfriend who by now is pregnant with their first child. I took the offer, easing himself into that decision with the thought that it is better to be a slave in heaven than a king in hell; the United States being heaven and Ghana being hell. The dumbest of analogies if there ever was any.

Thus I came to be hired to my first steady job in the US -- a floor worker earning less than "minimum" at a bakery in the Bronx. Nothing I had done in life to this point had prepared me for the first day on the job. It began with two trains and one bus trip from the Queens home to the factory in the Bronx. Here I joined a crew of fifteen floor workers for an eight-hour shift that started at 3 in the afternoon and ended at 11 deep night with a one-hour lunch break somewhere in between. Many in the group were French speaking Africans, a few English-speaking Africans, a couple of Jamaicans and a sprinkle of Mexican or South American guys. In fact the head man of the group was Abdul, a Malian. He spoke English and French very fluently. You needed no special expertise to tell that everyone was an undocumented immigrant; an "illegal alien" unauthorized to work in any capacity and therefore a ready source of cheap, cheap labor.

My work details consisted of :

1. arranging frozen bagels dough on trays to thaw and rise
2. Packing racks of baked pastries (donuts, bread, bagels, muffins etc.) into a freezer set at no less than twenty degrees below zero.
3. loading five huge trucks with baked pastries to be delivered overnight to restaurants for sale to the public the next morning.

All these I was required to perform without any relevant protective equipment such as insulated hand gloves, freezer clothing, boots, stools etc. Then there was the constant tongue lashing and insulting commands by Abdul the Malian who had made himself, to the delight of the white manager Ralph, a modern-day equivalent of a slave driver, *a head "N" in charge.*

Lunch break came and I had completed a little more than a quarter of the day's workload. It was evident that there was no way I would be done by the shift's end. Saviors came my way in the persons of William, a Ghanaian and Walter, a Jamaican. Both were old hands at the place. They had had taken note of my struggles and out of the goodness of their hearts, without being asked, offered to help pack the freshly baked pastries into the storage freezer. Walter the Jamaican greatly intrigued me. He spoke the most original street version of Jamaican Patwah almost to point of it sounding musical. It was by his influence that I came to incorporate Patwah expressions like *"bombo cla", "ras clas"* into my vocabulary bank without knowing them to be obscene street slangs.

As I sat my battered and beaten body on the train for the trip back home, I sobbed quietly, wondering how long I could endure the physical and emotional torture. Is this the American dream? This was more of an unfolding nightmare than a dream. Then again, I calculated my anticipated weekly earnings, converted them by "black market" exchange rate and talked myself into acceptance with the better a slave in heaven (America) than a king in hell (Ghana) nonsense.

I worked six days weekly and took home an average wage of about $180.00 for about nine months. Somewhere along, my hourly wage was humped by fifty cents to $3.75. As days turned into weeks and months, I could recite the names of all kinds of pastries, nuts and creams as well as muffins, donuts, cakes, breads, and anything in between that had the slightest drop of flour and sugar. All this while, I kept scouring employment pages of newspapers, New York Times and the Daily News in particular hoping to find something, anything that could take me away from flipping pastries, mopping freezers and cleaning ovens for slave wages. I found a way within myself to deal with the emotional turmoil related to how my life has changed. The physical battering was another thing all together. I kept searching for jobs that would not require so much physical stress, if even at a lesser remuneration. With my lady now pregnant with our first child conceived of bagels and muffins and cheesecake, it had become evident that a higher income was needed to support an emerging family of three. Then a friend, Kojo Andoh, told me about an opening at his workplace in the city, a Jewish-owned investment management firm on New York's Wall Street.

Once again, I proudly listed my educational credentials and work experience on the application form and once again was told what had been told me many times over. "Well, you are over-qualified for the opening I have. But you can have it if you don't mind". This time, the opening was for a messenger: job description -- stuff envelopes, prepare items for mass mailings, deliver mails to designated locations throughout the city, run business related errands as may be assigned by the supervisor; conditions -- forty hours weekly (Monday to Friday), regular work hours (nine to five), one-week unpaid vacation after one year, starting hourly wage of $5.50, promotion when available. That's how come I quit flipping bagels to working full time as a messenger at a financial business outfit on New York's Wall Street. To supplement my earnings, I went shopping and secured a part time job as a houseman at a prestigious hotel. I by now had heard the "over-qualified" refrain so often that it meant nothing when it was invoked once again. All I cared for was a much-needed extra income.

12

Authorized to Work

Perhaps one of the unwritten rules in the "illegal alien" underworld was never to ask anyone about his or her *"krataa"* or residency status. You don't ask because everyone is a legal resident, in the same manner that everyone in prison is innocent! Traveling in and out of the country is a solid way of telling intrusive and enquiring minds that you are legit. End of story!

Certain jobs, however, gave things away; jobs such as being a cab driver, security guard, hotel maid/houseman, working at fast food joints (KFC, McDonalds, Zaros, etc.), adult care (live-in/live-out), babysitting, supermarket cashier, store clerk. These are some of what you will be doing if you entered the US with a B1 visa that said, "employment unauthorized". You could secure neither a valid social security number nor an employment authorization certification that enabled you to look for work that matched your educational credentials and work experience. That is how come I and a Ghana Army officer, a Major, got acquainted with each other on floor and deep freezers at the bakery in the Bronx. I was supposedly visiting, and he was in the country for a training program and was using his free time to pick up a few extra nickels and dimes for himself. You might want to know what I was using the few free moments I had on Sundays to do. Myself and my partner were making babies. Our son Kobina was born in October, a year and one month removed from when I came.

Then in November 1986. President Ronald Reagan signed into law a statute that granted amnesty to illegal immigrants who entered the

United States before January 1, 1982 and had resided continuously, had not gone foul of the nation's laws or ever been on public support. The **Immigration Reform and Control Act (IRCA),** known famously as **Reagan Amnesty**, also granted legal status to certain seasonal agricultural workers living here illegally.

Claiming to belong in the latter category, I emptied my bank account, gathered documents supporting a claim to have once worked picking oranges on a commercial farm in the New York area and headed south to Florida, the citrus farming capital of the nation. Did I ever pick oranges on a commercial farm? The world would never know. I returned a week later with a one-year employment authorization card, renewable yearly. Not only could one legally work at any job, but I also now was on a clear path to acquiring the sacred green card and legal residency in no more than two years, barring any brushes with the laws of the land. Rather than a plane flight back, I opted to do the thirty hours train ride on Amtrak's Silver Star, hoping that it would give me a good opportunity to see much of the eastern corridor of the country. It did. It also gave me lots of idle time, time that would goad me to meditate on life and its travails. That's what a day and half train ride would do to you.

Between reading, sleeping, eating and gazing at the vegetation as the speeding train snaked its way up north, my mind sought for an explanation of how and why a person's life and fortunes have come to be determined by the possession of a mere plastic piece no larger than a business card. Isn't moving from place to place, migration, the "inalienable right" of all humans as is "life, liberty and pursuit of happiness"? How can it be that a humanoid can designate another "alien" on the planet they both share and forbid him to work to sustain himself?   What philosophy informs the idea that some forms of voluntary human movement from place to place is criminal and must be controlled and contained?

If humans started off as hunters and gatherers, it would seem tenable for them to be migrants, constantly on the move, hunting and gathering. Having been taught the story of the European man (i.e. History), I have consumed the narration of how he sailed the ocean valiantly battling the denizens of the wild and unknown to explore and civilize the world. 'Voyages of Exploration' was how it was titled in one high school textbook that bore the name "Makers of Civilization" which can be described as an exercise in the putrid subversion of truth to mask the heinous misdeeds of a bad neighbor. Stripped of niceties, they were European migration trails that would culminate in global conquests of unsuspecting populations.

I had studied how Europeans migrated to settle in far off places in Africa, Australia, the Americas and elsewhere. It is known that wherever they disembarked, the travel beaten and battered European migrants encountered native and entrenched populations who received them never imposed any residency requirements. Nana Kwamina Ansah, the chief of Edina, a tiny fishing village on the West African coast who took in a bunch of tired, storm beaten, scurvy ravaged, definitely famished Portuguese adventurers in or around 1472 never demanded any "krataa" or impose any residency conditions. Neither did the native Arawak who were the first native people of the so-called New World to encounter Christopher Columbus in 1492. Same can be said of the Aztecs who welcomed the Spanish 'Conquistadors', the Zulus of South Africa who took in the Dutch and British or the Australian Aborigines who passively allowed the British to settle their lands. Ironically, not only did the new arrivals settle, but they also subdued, conquered, enslaved and cynically attempted to exterminate the very natives who had welcomed and granted freedom to settle. Had they all singularly or collectively asked for green cards and visas perhaps, Africans would not have suffered the evil Trans-Atlantic slave trade and chattel slavery; native populations of America, Australia and elsewhere been slaughtered to the point of near genocidal extinction as history has them recorded.

Fast forward to the Twentieth Century and retell the story with roles reversed. This time it is an African migrant wanting to settle in a place controlled by European descendants. He is listed as an illegal, undocumented alien required to secure a plastic card before he could work to sustain himself. You can't make this up!

With the card in hand, it felt like I had just been let out of jail, born-again, a free bird released to soar the skies in pursuit of the fabled American dream. Not so fast, though. One would have to navigate the intricate maze of relationships in the country – religious, racial, economic, etc. Authorized to work did not confer a license or freedom to work at where and what one so desire. I interviewed for assistant manager's position at two hotels, applied for office operations positions. Administrative assistant at banks and came away with blanks. So months after having been authorized to work, yours sincerely continued working nine to five, Monday to Friday as a messenger, and on weekends as a houseman at this prestigious Marriot Marquis hotel in midtown New York City.

Then one day, I stumbled onto a news report on shortage of qualified teachers in specialized areas -- science, mathematics and special education and that New York City Education Department was hiring persons with bachelors' degrees who would work in those shortage areas in the school system. The department would grant scholarships for advanced degree studies as well as sponsor qualified "illegals" for lawful residency in the country for those who would commit themselves to teach for two years.

My bachelor's degree from the University of Cape Coast fitted me perfectly for the job. And that is how come in February 1989, a little over two years since arriving in the country, I was hired as a "permanent per diem" (a glorified "pupil teacher") in the New York City school system. It would be the first time that the wages I earned would be commensurate in a measure to my educational credentials and work experience.

Either by reason of self-assured arrogance, exceptionalism or both, the United States does not give unqualified recognition to any foreign credentials. You will be required to undergo some form of American training to be recognized as such. In other words, if one intended to teach in American schools, one would have to acquire American academic and professional credentials for teaching in American schools.

I enrolled in a part time master's degree program paid for through the scholarship granted by my employers. I worked full time Monday to Friday and attended classes in the evenings as well as all day Saturdays and Sundays. On weekends, I would drive about twenty-five miles to leave my infant son in the care of a friend Joyce's house. Good old Aunt Joyce, a long-standing friend whose heart overflows with love and kindness had agreed to baby-sit at no cost while I attended classes to graduate eighteen months later with a master's degree in special education and psychology.

13

Green Carded Visit to Ghana

Once you became legal, you wanted to flaunt it by taking a trip out of the country. That way you would quietly announce your changed status and be admitted into the circle of those who naively saw themselves as part of this great "land of the free and the home of the brave". The airs around you changed as did the ground on which you walked, a feeling that consumed you when you got your first visa. Sounds funny and surreptitiously stupid. But it is true.

Five months after being authorized to work, I packed myself and my two years old son for a trip back to the "green, green grass of home". Back to Ghana, that is.

The six-week vacation was as heavenly as it was memorable. We were received and treated as a home coming princes by family, friends and all. The infant Koby, however got the most attention and adoration. His every action and reaction were seen as either funny or weird viewed within the context of how the homefolks do things. One of his favorite pass times consisted of chasing fowls and chickens as if they were playmates in the park. He also on several occasions attempted to hitch a piggyback ride of the house dog. Of course he fell each time and announced his righteous frustration in temper tantrums and tears. Inexplicably, the dog never barked or moved away, not even once. She stood and tolerated Koby's abuses as a mother would her puppies. Not once did she bark, stomp or even move away from the boy. It was indeed fascinating to watch Hope (that's the dog's name) literally invite the kid to do onto her what she would not permit anyone else to do unto her.

Was it due to him being a baby or was it because Hope somehow knew Koby was just visiting?

I came home one day after an outing on the town and walked into the loudest tantrum that my son had ever thrown. Over what? Abla, the house help had given Koby a bath and wanted to slip him into one of his old jeans. The boy had other ideas and preferred something else, a new outfit that still had all the labels and the $9.99 price tag attached. Yelling, crying and kicking, he fought against attempts to put the old jeans on his tiny body. Abla understandably was frustrated and scared, thinking she would be accused of having assaulted the kid. Koby leapt into my arms and between sobs, attempted to tell his dad what the issue was in his "guggul gaga meme mama" babyish drawl.

Abla explained: "He wouldn't wear the old jeans. He wants the new one which has not been opened".

"Is that all the reason for this mighty confusion?", I asked.

"Yes, Daddy"

"But the new one is his. So why won't you let him have it?"

"It is new. It has not been opened", said Abla.

"It's okay. Just let him have it. It is his to wear. And its only $9.99".

Like Abla, a dumbfounded grandmother, Maama, shook her and muttered:

"As for you these *Abrokyiri* people, that is why your children are so spoilt! Keep them there. Don't bring them here o!"

This trip would be the last time I would see my mother alive and well. She would die six years later, a victim of heart failure brought on by several years battle with high blood pressure and a cardiovascular ailment. When time came for father and son to return to the States, the ordeal we endured at Ghana's airport was enough to wipe away all memories of the warmth and fun we had enjoyed during the six weeks stay.

It was the peak period of a dreadful "revolution" in Ghana. A young soldier named Jerry Rawling had orchestrated a violent overthrow of the country's government. His bitter disgust (in a way justified) with the country's leadership had garnered the support of the entire nation, especially the youth. He and his band of gun totting colleagues meant to purge the land of ills and woes brought on essentially through the deeds and misdeeds of leaders of the time. That those leaders were corrupt and inept could neither be denied nor contested. They had woefully mismanaged the country's affairs and resources and gutted its ability to guarantee development, freedom, justice and equal opportunities for all. A wild and spontaneous uprising of the youth ensued.

As it is with mass uprisings, it didn't take long for the laudable objectives of the purge to degenerate into a rudderless search for how to reach those goals.

The young revolutionaries launched what appeared to be an assault on corruption and mis application of public wealth. Caught in an obsessive fit to undo the massive damage done the nation by preceding administrations, they employed brutal tactics to pull down physical structures and exacted bloody retribution to punish those adjudged to have committed "crimes against the people". They demolished and pulled down buildings and physical structures but did not offer much of sound strategies to repair, reform and rebuild. Knee jerk decision and actions understandably created fear and uncertainty within and alarmed enemies without. Western neo-colonial interests put the squeeze on. Shortages of life essentials incubated and delivered a fresh brand of corruption and thievery, the very ails the "revolution" was intended to purge. Not only did corruptible practices prevail, but they became much more invasive, evasive, and sophisticated.

Those whose duty it was to oversee fair and equitable access to life's essentials such as water, food, transportation, health care etc. squeezed them for personal gains. The international airport in the Accra became a stinking cesspool of corrupt practices, it being the only facility for international travel in and out of the country. Maneuvering the many procedural encumbrances that had been unnecessarily and illegally contrived was perhaps more difficult and frustrating than finding one's way out of the Pharaoh's burial chamber within the pyramid of Giza! What else could one expect in a country plagued by acute shortages of nearly everything from toilet paper to parchment paper and pain killer to female sanitary napkin.

By the time we cleared every obstacle and got to the boarding gate, anger and frustration had condensed into beads of sweat on my body parts and unceasing tears on my boy's face, making me bitterly regret the decision to go visit the homeland with my son. Crooked airline personnel, immigration/custom officials, baggage carriers and others under a so-called revolutionary dispensation had done their due! A very exhausted and angry me kicked my feet at the airplane's gate and muttered to himself : "Revolution, kiss my ass! Take your Ghana".

14

Cold Encounter on a New Jersey Highway

Its December 1998, fifteen years after I entered the United States. I had acquired its citizenship, comfortably settled with a good job, wife and three lovely children -- two girls and a boy. I had a huge presence in the African/Ghanaian immigrant community derived mainly from my participation and service towards community organization and activism.

Ghanaians in the area had gotten into the business of organizing themselves into identifiable legal entities allowable by the country's laws. By the 1990s, a sizeable (by African standards but insignificant by American demographics) community of Ghanaians was emerging in the country. It has been growing steadily in numbers from the 1970s. Each decade, the numbers doubled and by 2015, the US Census Bureau listed over a hundred thousand Ghanaians to be living in the United States. This includes naturalized citizens, lawful permanent residents, refugees and asylees, legal non-immigrants (including those on student, work, or other temporary visas), and persons residing in the country without authorization. It is widely believed (with good reason) that a good chunk of these lived in the greater New York-New Jersey-Connecticut metropolitan area.

Driven by the nostalgia, need for identity, belongingness, a number of ethnically based cultural organizations began to form. In the New York metro area at least ten of such groups were legally incorporated and functional by 1985. They included Akan Association, Asanteman Association, Akyem Association, Ga-Dangme Kpee*, Okuapemman

Fekuw*, Ewe Haborbor*, Nzema Association, Ewe Unity Club, Yankassa Association, etc. Each of these groups were ethno-linguistically based, meaning they were made up of people from the one district of Ghana and who spoke the same language -- Akan Association for coastal Fante speakers, Asanteman for indigenous Ashanti, Akyem for indigenous Akyems, Ga-Dangme for Gas/Krobos, Ewe Unity/Haborbor for Ewe speakers, Okuapemman for Akuapems, Nzema for speakers of Nzema and Yankassa for persons from the northern regional area of Ghana. A few more tribal groups would come into being in later years ---- Amansie Kuo*, Brong Ahafo Association, Mfantse Ebusua Kuw, Ablade, Ada Okorbi, Kwakwaduam, etc. I joined the Okuapemman Fekuw in 1987 and was instantly elected to be its Secretary.

All of these entities had similar, if not identical, aims and purposes namely: unify people from the area, provide avenues for socialization, project unique culture markers, support one another when the need arises (during major transitional occurrences such as births, deaths, retirements, relocations, etc.) They all held monthly general meetings on where they expressed themselves verbally and behaviorally by their inherent cultural traditions. Some, like the Asanteman Association, Ewe Haborbor and Mfantse Ebusua Kuw adopted traditional Ghanaian leadership models in their organizational structures. Elected leaders such as presidents, secretaries assumed reverential royal titles -- *Nana, Togbe, Nii, Nanahemaa,* etc. styling themselves in manners of dressing, speech, public appearances, as traditional leaders (i.e. chiefs) do back in Ghana.

In time, leaders of the fledging ethnic groupings woke up to the duplicitous nature of their aims, objectives and activities. In the summer of 1985, therefore, leaders of eleven of the existing major associations at the time met to chart a unification course. From this initial meeting emerged an organization that would embrace all of them into a single body while leaving room for each to retain its independent existence and authority. It would be the coordinated voice or spokesperson for all matters of common interests to Ghanaians. A draft constitution was adopted in January 1986. The newly minted National Council of Ghanaian Associations Incorporated (acronym NCOGA), became at that time the only one of its kind formed by citizens of any African country residing outside continental Africa.

NCOGA is organized and operated on the same principles as the UN. The chief administrative officers are the Executive Secretary General (ESG) and the Deputy Executive Secretary General (DESG). They run a Secretariat responsible for the day-to-day administration of the Council. I would at different times be elected to both ESG and DESG positions.

It was within these times that I and my dear friend Dr George Lamptey founded a community news magazine, **The Asenta**, a hugely successful venture that flourished for seven years before folding. I first met George in the meeting halls of NCOGA. Our friendship took off right away and over the years made us into brothers, not by blood, but through the telepathic inter connectedness of our thoughts, ideas and dreams. We have come to share joy, successes, tears and disappointments like blood brothers. AfriComm Inc, the publishing corporation we founded had to fold when the *9/11 terror attacks* happened and we lost most of our advertising sponsors. Though it went down with thousands of dollars in financial losses and shattered credit history, my life and health stayed sound, thanks largely to my wife Florence, giving me a chance to bounce back to repair what had been destroyed.

In December 1999, a friend who lived in West Orange, New Jersey, lost his wife in a tragic vehicular accident. It was a Christmas eve tragedy whose pain and grieve was felt throughout the entire Ghanaian community and even as far as back as across the home continent.

A heavy snowstorm hit the area, blanketing the area with several inches of the white stuff. In line with a long-standing tradition of sorts, the Ghanaian community in northern New Jersey, had scheduled its annual year-end party for that evening at the city of Newark. With no snow-out plans on tap, the show had to go on as planned. A recovering drug-addict-ex con drove an uninsured car into a group of party goers, instantly killing two ladies right in front of the hall where the party was holding.

An hour and half's drive away, I sat relaxed, taking in the late-night TV news when call of the accident came. I picked myself up and drove to my friend's home, intending to console and keep him company. The temperature was several degrees below freezing but I was not heavily bundled up (as I should have), a miscalculation that very nearly cost me my life. I wore a light trench coat over a shirt and pants with a fedora hat to match. After all I drove a well-maintained car with its temperature controls and all other conveniences functioning as they should.

I stayed overnight. Around midnight of the next day, I slipped comfortably into the driver's seat to begin what I thought was going to be a normal hour and half drive back to my home base to spruce myself for work the next morning. I had gone thirty minutes when I noticed the engine temperature gauge rising, a tell-tale sign that the engine was overheating. Intending to go back, I made a quick about turn. But the car could go no further than about five hundred meters up a steep incline. It stalled right in the middle of a country road on the coldest night of the season with temperature in the teens. And all I had for protection against the elements was a trench coat and a fedora hat! Steam poured out of the boiling radiator with a loud hissing sound. I stood in the biting cold wondering what to do. It did not take long for me to lose feel of my fingers, toes, ears, lips and nose. I must have blackened out because when I came to, I was sitting in the back of a car with a man and woman in the front. They both were of Asian extraction, probably Chinese.

"How are you feeling?", the man asked.

I nodded, as to say "better". My lips could not form and sound the words. They were too frost-bitten.

"I saw you drop to the ground. Do you remember what happened"?

I shook my head as in "no".

"I pulled you in. It's too cold to be out there. You lucky we showed up".

They had my feet and hands wrapped in what seemed to be blankets. They deliberately had lowered the temperature in the car. He explained that with my near frozen condition, a sudden exposure to high heat could shock the body system and cause severe damage to vital organs.

After what seemed like eternity, I slowly began to feel more and more rejuvenated in my body parts.

The man said they had visited his mother-in-law but had inexplicably missed the exit to their home!

"That's just how we came by you", the man said.

He then pulled out a cell phone and called 911 and called for emergency assistance. Mind you, cell phones at this time were novelties that few could afford. I wasn't of the few. Minutes later, a police officer and emergency medical service people showed up. They collectively had me patched up and the car towed to a garage. I had slipped through what would have been an icy death caused by hypothermia. You know, humans are warm blooded animals, meaning their body temperature is not, by and large, adversely altered by the temperature of their surroundings. But in extreme situations, the body is unable to generate heat fast enough to replenish what it loses. Hypothermia, a medical condition of dangerously low body temperature which can cause death sets in. Icy death!

As much as I tried, the couple declined to give me any information about themselves -- name, telephone number, address, nothing. I want to hope that they are alive and well somewhere in the town of West Orange in New Jersey State.

15

Community Service

Between 1990 and 2014, I spent an inordinate amount of my time, talents and treasures in voluntary service to the African/Ghanaian immigrant community. There were times that I served as the General Secretary of Okuapemman Fekuw (Association); Deputy Executive Secretary General (DESG) and Executive Secretary General (ESG) of the National Council of Ghanaian Associations (NCOGA); member Pan African Development Organization (PADO); member African Community Leaders Committee under New York City Mayor David Dinkins. Being a co-founder , Editor-in-Chief and Publisher of the Asenta News Magazine with presence in twenty-eight states, one would rake in extensive travel miles while writing countless editorials and commentaries on matters of topical interest to African people.

In the inter twining years, I enjoyed what I consider to be the most fulfilling, certainly not the happiest, years of my earthly existence. I served the African/Ghanaian immigrant community in the New York-Connecticut-New Jersey area with dedication and passion that I had hitherto reserved exclusively for my family and own socio-economic mobility and advancement. I literally pushed them to the side so I could attend to community concerns. Needless to say I lost quite a bit on family fun and career advancement.

A large African community had emerged and needed its fair share of the national cake. We needed media exposure, economic opportunities, fair treatment by law enforcement agents, access to political power and the sharpening of our social consciousness and responsibilities.

Fate thrusted me into non-profit, non-political advocacy organizations such as the National Council of Ghanaian Associations (NCOGA) and the Pan African Development Organization (PADO). Center for African Initiatives (CAI), Society for American Ghanaian Educators (SAGES), Ghana Cultural School Inc, OBS World USA Inc, Lefrak City Ghanaian Benevolent Association are those I co-founded and served voluntarily. I took on assignments that had me engage with visiting African politicians and resident diplomats as well as elected American office holders. I held the microphone for persons who must be heard, amongst them UN Secretary General Kofi Annan, Ghana Presidents J.J Rawlings, John Kuffour, Atta Mills and John Mahama. Working with several heads of Ghana's diplomatic missions was a source of great learning with satisfaction.

I did news reports and hosted talk shows on radio and television, recorded volumes of minutes of all manner of meetings, wrote countless articles and commentaries, gave speeches and made presentations on matters of topical importance to us. When not in the thick of a parade or protest for social justice, one could be found negotiating resolutions of conflicts such as police harassment or immigration reforms.

By reason of an exceptional ability to blend words with humor, I earned immense recognition and respect for excellence in emceeing all types of public events – dinner dances, anniversaries, weddings, funerals, picnics, name it. I led work teams that promoted African ventures such as Ghana Airways, Ghana Real Estate Development Association (GREDA) and others in entertainment, tourism, cultural education/exchange, sports and commerce throughout the country.

My service to the community derives from a deep seated desire to make the community better than I found it without any monetary compensation. It remains my calling till I exit this plain. Still, it had its rewards. What I sacrificed in monetary compensation and career advancement, I reaped hundred folds in societal recognition, intellectual growth, spiritual enrichment and personal fulfillment.

**Ushering then UN Secretary General Kofi Annan
into a community event in his honor.**

**Introducing Ghana's President John Mahama
to community leaders in New York**

**Camera moment with Ghana President John Atta Mills
at a New York Ghanaian community event**

**A picture moment with Ghana President John Agyekum Kuffour
at a reception in his honor in New York**

**Welcoming Ghana Ambassador to the United States
Alan Kyerematen to a community event**

**In discussion with Ghana Ambassador to the
UN Ken Kanda, left, and community leader Patrick Gyan.**

**Assisting Ghanaian Minister of State Nana Oye Lithur
to honor community leader Dr Kofi Boateng**

Interviewing Dr Tony Aidoo

Emceeing a community event

Offering traditional libational prayers at Ghana flag raising
ceremony at Yonkers City Hall to honor
Ghana's independence anniversary

Eulogizing a late friend at Rev Dr Obiri Addo's church
Calling punches with boxing legend Oscar de la Hoya

A slate of distinguished diplomats that I had the honor and privilege to meet and work with in service to our diaspora community: James Gbeho, Dr George Lamptey, Dr Kofi Awoonor, Nana Effa Apenteng, Mrs Akyaa Pobee, Koby Koomson, Ekow Spio Garbrah, Allan Kyerematten, Jack Wilmot, Leslie Kojo Christian, Ken Kanda, Martha Pobee, William Awinador-Kanyirige, Ernest Lomotey, Adotey Anum, Joe Ackon, Kwesi Arhin, Kwesi Quantson and many others whose names time has blotted from memory's pages

16

Clinically Dead in New York

I went back to working in the New York public school system in 1999 with a few hundred thousand in credit card bills in tow. My credit had been shot to the point where no carrier would grant me a mere cell phone. Ten years passed and I had managed to turn the corner as far my finances go. My wife convinced herself all in possible ways that I am a filthy adulterous philander. My children grew up torn between believing what they heard mother said and what they saw me do as a doting, very caring father and family man. I drifted back into the old boring routine of work from 8 a.m. to 3 p.m. Monday to Friday, Saturday evenings social actions like parties and Sunday occasional church attendance. We lived through and survived the 9/11/2001 Terrorist attack on the United States as well as storms and blizzards notably the Blizzard of December 1999.

Then came the hot and hazy morning of July 22, 2014. It was a quiet Tuesday morning, flush in the middle of summer. The air was still, no birds sang, and no flags swung in the wind. The heavens would not betray what was to come. Cataclysmic events, it is said, are preceded by flags fluttering in the wind. Not this one.

I was the last to leave home to go to the summer teaching job I had taken on. The vacation job brought in some good extra penny.

It must have been around 11:10 a.m. The second class of Math students for the day had just settled in. That was when consciousness ended for me and gloom and doom took over. Everything I write from this point on are based on accounts given me by some of the great number of individuals who were there and saw it all --- principal, assistant principals, colleagues, students, my exceptionally good friend Dr Kofi Adu, my wife Florence, my kids Asabea, Koby and Bedua, doctors and nurses at Mount Sinai hospitals in Queens and Manhattan.

The Math class had barely settled in when I complained that I wasn't feeling too well and pulled a chair intending to sit. I tumbled over and fell limp. I had suffered a massive cardiac attack or heart attack. My heart had stopped beating and my breath had ceased. Hysteria and pandemonium broke loose among these teenagers. They ran out of the room, some screaming "Mr. Anor is dying, Mr. Anor is dying". Others ran to the Principal's office for help.

Mr. Clemente Lopes hurried to the room with his assistant Alfredo and the school nurse in tow. They had a defibrillator which the school kept on site mainly for asthma and other breathing emergencies. Being an ex-army officer. Mr. Lopes knew exactly what to do. He proceeded to administer cardiac pulmonary resuscitation (CPR) while the nurse checked for vital signs. They administered five shocks to my heart. Before then, he cleared the room of all students. He knew me to be an immensely proud man who would not want the world to know that my bowels have opened up when I fell unconscious.

Alfredo called for 911 emergency medical help provided through the City's Emergency Medical Service (EMS). Thanks to the CPR administered by Mr. Lopes and his expert manipulation of the defibrillator, my heart which had stopped beating began fluttering like a stutterer struggling to make a point before a court judge. It would start and stop. Precious minutes which seemed like eternity passed and no ambulance had showed up. Out desperation Alfredo stepped outside in hope of commandeering one driving by. And that was exactly what happened. Alfredo flagged down a passing ambulance and literally hijacked it to where I laid. His craziness had paid off! The EMS personnel took over and had me taken to the nearest and best hospital in the area -- Mount Sinai Queens. All this while I had become comatose, also known in medical terms as a "clinically dead". Between the EMS and Emergency Room personnel, I was given additional six shocks, making a total of eleven. My heart was all but gone. The brain was what kept me alive. I was *clinically dead.** The doctors made the call.

Clinical death is said to occur when the heart stops beating in a regular rhythm and there is cessation of blood circulation and breathing. It is synonymous with there being no medical signs of life -- no breathing, no pulse, no heartbeat -- a condition called cardiac arrest. At the onset of clinical death, consciousness is lost within several seconds. Measurable brain activity stops within 20 to 40 seconds.

In the mid-morning hours of July 22, 2014, all these conditions applied to me. The doctors decided to "shut down" all other organs except the brain. With the heart spluttering that much, only a very miniscule amount of oxygenated blood was being made available for the entire body system. With all others disabled, the brain which is most vital of all vital organs in the human body will become the main recipient of whatever oxygenated blood came in and minimize the possibility of the brain sustaining any ischemic injury. Thus did I come to be immersed neck down in an ice encasement. Mount Sinai Queens had done what was in their power to do. Their machines would keep me comatose till death came.

Such was my state that when my wife, Florence, first laid eyes on me she fainted and had to be admitted into the same emergency room I had been held initially. Two for the price of one!

Still, a critical decision needed to be made. It involved the risky business of whether to move me to a bigger and better facility in Manhattan, a two-hour drive away. Though not guaranteed, there was a chance that I could be saved there. The chance also existed that they would lose me while moving me back and forth. On the other hand, keeping me in Queens meant I would be stay comatose until such time as the brain would go until absolute, irreversible death sets in.

Unto Florence, my wife, our children Asabea, Koby and Bedua fell the grim responsibility of making the call. On the advice of Dr Kofi Adu, himself an accomplished surgeon and the finest friend anyone could be blessed to have, they opted to risk taking me to Manhattan. If I made it, fine. If I didn't, so what? I would die in Queens anyway.

As fate would have it, I made it to Manhattan and to a chance of being saved.

I remained comatose in the Critical Care Unit of the hospital for four days, kept alive by tubes attached to all sorts of machines and monitors. My limp body coupled with the pings and beeps these critical equipment made served to remind visitors about man's limitations and the frailty of life.

My miracle came complete when on the fourth day, the heart began beating once again! It was sudden and unexpected. Koby had taken my hand just as he did anytime, he came to the beside. He casually said "Dad, squeeze my hand if you hear me". He saw my finger twitch ever so feebly, an indication that I heard him and was trying to comply. He yelled out a shout of joyous excitement. "He is alive!" My journey back had begun. The heart that would not respond to any electrical stimulations suddenly came alive. The emergence from coma had begun. By the fifth day, a Saturday and my soul day, I was completely conscious but physically weak and drained. I could ask / answer questions and in my signature style, actually share a joke or two!

The next few days would be used to ascertain the extent of damage , if any, done to any and all of my body organs. Then a determination would be made as to what to do about them. The doctors were most worried about the brain. The law of averages in their profession concerning my prognosis indicated that the brain would sustain some form of damage which would in turn adversely affect my performance in speech mobility, cognition, etc. There was a real chance that any one or more of these may have suffered damage that could be reversible or otherwise. In the meantime, contingency plans made up of varying levels of therapeutic rehabilitations were drawn up to deal with whatever might crop up. So began a sleuth of tests, x-rays, scans and what have you. No matter how many times they were done, they all came back negative. Incredible! Unbelievable! Miraculous! Strange! Unreal! Inexplicable! These are some of the words I heard repeated over and over again, by scientists whose work and world revolves entirely around facts supported by empirical evidence. Not only have I survived a massive cardiac arrest. I have come out of it with all my brain power and capabilities solidly intact!

One morning , a team of doctors and nurses showed up at my bedside for the usual examinations. They were having a hard time finding a vein in my arm to draw blood. My arm has been pinched and pricked so many times!

Calmly, I offered a suggestion thus: "Can't find a vein? Go downstairs. There is a big one dangling between my legs". The room exploded with laughter. Then somebody said "Damn, this man is all right. Nothing's wrong with him."

One week after the tussle with death had begun, it ended as swiftly as it started. I was let go from the hospital with stents inserted into blocked arteries to straighten them out, a defibrillator (pacemaker) in the chest to jump start the heart anytime it decided to sleep on the job, a cache of medications and a long slate of do's and don'ts which included eating heart healthy diet, exercising, abstaining from sex (especially with girl friends; it's too exciting there! -- according to my cardiologist), avoiding stress, quit smoking (if I do, which I didn't), cutting down on salt and alcohol, keeping up with all your doctor's appointments etc., etc.

Dr. Adu and his wife Margaret whisked me to their pad in a quiet up state town called Monsey so I could recuperate in nature and quietude, far away from the madding crowd of New York City.

As I write, I have kept faith with most, if not all of these injunctions. Now I exercise and go on long walks all by myself after my wife and kids had graciously started me off on short round-the-block trips.

About four months after hospital discharge, I marked my miraculous survival with a church service and invited all my family, friends and loved ones join me make a joyful and thankful noise unto God. It seemed everyone was there, except for those whose petty souls would not permit them. Regretfully, it included some awfully close family members. If ever there was a miracle, I have had mine and who else could be responsible for it? A church to me is the best place to go to find and thank the God who made it happen.

I went back to work two weeks after, believing that I was mended well enough mentally and physically to handle the rumble and tumble of working with young teenagers in a school. I couldn't be terribly mistaken. Three months after resuming work, in March 2015, I suffered another heart attack, again on the job and at the same location, albeit a mild one. This time, I did not lose consciousness. I spent four days in the hospital. Tests revealed blockage in a different artery. A stent is inserted to unblock it, bringing the total in me to four.

It brought into my focus two stark facts of life -- 1. all things mortal has a terminal point; 2. there are only opportunities, no guarantees. I could not remain employed forever. Neither was I assured of recovering from another attack at the same location or anywhere else. The question then was "to retire or not to retire"? And live the remaining years of my life to and for me and my loved ones? After nearly twenty-seven years in the employ of the New York City government, one could retire with very decent benefits and entitlements.

So I retired on the First of July 2015, nearly a year away from the day that I died clinically but was granted a reprieve and pulled back through the efforts of men and women guided by what I strongly believe to be a Power far beyond the understanding of man.

Prior to the middle of the 20th century, the absence of blood circulation and vital functions related to blood circulation was considered to be the definition of death. With advances in medicine, it is possible to reverse cardiac arrest through cardiopulmonary resuscitation (CPR), defibrillation and other treatments to restore normal heartbeat and circulation. Instead of death, cardiac arrest came to be called "clinical death", meaning the clinical appearance of death. Clinical death is now seen as a medical condition that precedes death rather than actually being dead. During clinical death, all tissues and organs in the body steadily accumulate a type of injury called ischemic injury.

EPILOGUE

Only two percent of persons who suffer cardiac arrests survive. I know a few who do not count among this lucky few. Mr. Asare Djan was the first Ghanaian Comptroller of Customs and Excise after independence. He was also my maternal uncle. He must have been in his early fifties when driving on the streets of Accra, he felt unbearably thirsty. He pulled up at a water stand. He died where he sat behind the steering wheel within minutes before the water got to him. Cause of death — heart attack.

At forty-eight, Mr. Ernest Kwaku Ayeh Dartey was a young, phenomenally successful entrepreneur. He was also my cousin. He was the first general manager of Black Star Lines shipping company Nkrumah established on a model created by Marcus Garvey, one of the foremost pan-Africanist of his time. Ernest left Black Star Lines and went on to co-found the Volta Lines, also a shipping company. He is relaxing at home with wife and kids one Sunday afternoon after church. He steps out to go the bathroom right across the hallway. He doesn't make it that far. He collapses and dies in the hallway right before his wife and kids. Heart attack had done its darndest.

Kwame Sandy lived and worked in the United States for most of his adult life until he located temporarily to Ghana to take up a top government job. He was a very well-liked and popular young man in the Ghanaian community in New York. Driving home from a meeting, he loses consciousness, and the car runs into a ditch somewhere between Osu and Labadi, suburbs of Accra, Ghana's capital city. He is rushed to a hospital where he is declared dead on arrival from a heart attack.

My particularly good friend Lawrence, a fun loving forty-nine-year young man full of life and vim is found dead in his room. He died overnight in his sleep. Autopsy report -- heart ailment.

Douglas Osei is one thoughtful and deliberate Ghanaian I ever knew, sometimes to the point of being cynical and annoying with his analysis and opinions. He steps out of his Lefrak City, Queens apartment for his usual evening walk. Alarm bells go off when by midnight he hadn't returned home. It is very unlike him. Morning breaks and still no sign of him. The police call later in the day to say that his body had been found about a quarter mile from his home. His driver's license helped identify him. A massive heart attack killed him.

Kwame Kennedy, popularly known as 'Kwame K' lived in Yonkers, NY with his wife and daughter. One Saturday winter night in 2013, he pays a courtesy visit to a friend in another part of town to help mourn the death of a mother in Ghana. Kwame K leaves at around midnight to go home. If only he knew that the grim reaper is coming for him where his car was parked. He collapses as he attempts to open the car door and dies then and there. Autopsy says he died from a heart attack.

An up-and-coming young doctor detours into a rest stop on a New York highway to use the bathroom. He is unable to step away from the steering wheel. Minutes later, he is found dead right where he sat, victim of a heart ailment.

Anthony Mason, a retired New York Knicks basketball team legend and a paradigm of strength and athletic prowess, collapses and dies suddenly, a young man in his forties -- a victim of cardiac arrest.

Komla Dumor, a celebrated journalist of international repute collapses and dies within minutes, at home, right in the prime of his life , an apparent victim of a heart attack.

In fact, heart attacks and other heart related ailments are listed as the number causes of death among middle aged men in the United States, perhaps throughout the world. It claims an estimated seventeen million lives worldwide each year.

I count as one of the very few of all those who die clinically from heart attacks and survive. Many are those who do not survive the initial jolt. Those who receive some kind of attention within minutes of the initial attack do not make it beyond five shocks to jump start the heart. I took eleven.

The human heart is not designed to splutter for days without causing irreparable damage to itself or vital organs like the brain, so says medical science. It is not a *"dumsor*-powered"* gadget. One year counting and all seem to be very well with me. My brain remains as sharp as ever, maybe sharper. I continue to think, talk and walk perhaps better than before. Ischemic injuries, where is thy victory?

Why me? What accounts for me being one of the lucky few? Who or what chose me? What accounts for **ME** being deserving of God's favor?

My befuddled doctors say for things to conclude the way to go the way it did for me, all the elements had to line up exactly the way they did -- appropriate first aid (Principal Clemente), on the spot professional attention (EMS personnel hijacked by Crazy Alfredo), a well-equipped medical facility manned by highly trained and competent personnel (Mount Sinai Queens and Manhattan). Had any one of these been out of place, I would be swimming with the fishes!

The "what ifs" are many and frightening. What if I had collapsed at home that Tuesday morning with no one around; or I collapsed while driving to work or Mr. Lopes wasn't around or did not know what to do with a defibrillator and "Crazy" Alfredo hadn't literally hijacked an ambulance? What if I was taken to another hospital in the area, and Dr Khan was not on hand at the Queens Mount Sinai facility to "shut" down my body organs to conserve blood to keep my brain working? What if we had run into notorious New York traffic jams and Mount Sinai did not turn out to be one of the best state of the art medical facilities in the country, nay the world?

Was it merely a coincidence that everything lined up as they did? Who jump-started the heart after it had ceased working for hours and days? Perhaps it was a lucky roll of the dice, my destiny or a sheer act of divine intervention by ancestral spirits, a guardian spirit and or by God Almighty.

I choose to believe that it's all of the above. Luck and destiny have their places in the scheme of things. But God's power trumps all things. My dearly departed mother and other good folks may be up there, shielding my spirit from pestilences that strike by day and by night. All duly acknowledged.

But I believe the ultimate divine intervention came from *God (English), Nyame (Akan), Allah (Arabic), Mawu (Ewe), Olorun (Yoruba), Chuwku (Igbo), Yahweh (Hebrew),* whatever you call yours. The final call is His to make. I do not know why I found favor in His sight. That's why I went to church to express my sincerest gratitude to Him, Her or It, Creator of heaven and Earth and all things within. I have been raised to believe in the existence of Being, the knowledge of which transcends human understanding. To deny this fact would count me among fools who say in their hearts that there is no God. My mother did not raise a fool!

Whereas before I died clinically my faith in the power and presence of the Supreme Being had been shaky and suspect, now it is solid and firm. Whereas I felt invincible, now I acknowledge my vulnerability. Whereas I felt confident in my own skin and prowess, now I admit to my mortal limitations. Whereas I used to see death as an inevitable proposition, now I accept it as being so near, awed by its unpredictability, fully aware that it will come when it must. I am dwarfed by my frailty in the presence of it all.

I live on fearlessly, one minute at a time, in supreme faith, trust and confidence in the God who wrestled me, more than once, out of the cold grasp of the grim reaper and gave me several chances at life. These are my miracles.

Before New York, there was me and my small nuclear family living a modestly happy life in Cape Coast. Here we are in 1969. Sitting from left: Papa Kwaku Anor (Patriach), Mama Yaa Asabea (Matriach). Standing left to right: Kwabena Opare (Theo), Akua Anorbea (Janet) carrying Baby Joana, Cousin Kwame Darko (DK), Kwabena Amoah (Gid), Ama Gyanmea (Emy), Kwame Ofori (Gad)